On Reconciliation

On Reconciliation

What Israelis and Palestinians Can Learn from South Africa and Rwanda

Maya Savir

Translated from the Hebrew by Todd Hasak-Lowy

Foreword by Aziz Abu Sarah

Plough

Published by Plough Publishing House
Walden, New York
Robertsbridge, England
Elsmore, Australia
www.plough.com

ISBN 978-1-63608-209-7
29 28 27 26 1 2 3 4

A catalog record for this book is available from the British Library.
Library of Congress Cataloging-in-Publication Data pending.

Printed in the United States of America

To my children.
I love you endlessly.

And now I have to confess the unpardonable and
the scandalous, in an age which scorns happiness.
I am a happy man.
And I am going to tell you the secret of my happiness.
It is quite simple. I love mankind. I love love. I hate hate.
I try to understand and accept.

Jean Cocteau

Contents

Foreword

Aziz Abu Sarah

AS A PALESTINIAN in East Jerusalem, I grew up believing that peace was impossible. My brother Tayseer died after being tortured by Israeli soldiers in 1991. He was nineteen years old, and I was ten. I grew up angry, believing that vengeance was justice. I couldn't imagine peace or reconciliation in our region. As Maya Savir explains in this book, we cannot use the logic of war and conflict when envisioning peace. It was eight years before I began to unlearn the logic of revenge, aggression, and hate. I had to go through a transformative journey to understand the logic of peacemaking. That journey started on the day that, for the first time in my life, as a young adult, I met an Israeli Jew who spoke to me as an equal and listened to my story. In the years since, I've learned that forgiveness is not easy; it is not even simply an emotional decision. It is something I had to train both my heart and my mind to embrace. It's a decision I still have to hold on to every day.

I have now worked with bereaved families on both sides of this conflict for almost three decades. I was first introduced to Maya by Maoz Inon, an Israeli Jew whose parents were killed by Hamas on October Seventh. Maoz has become a brother to me; together we wrote the book *The Future Is Peace*, and Maya is one of the people we interviewed while writing the book. In Israel, Maoz always carries Hebrew copies of Maya's book in his backpack, to give anyone who will read it. I know some are inclined to dismiss this book because it was written by an

Israeli Jew, but this Israeli Jew is my sister in peace, and I hope you are able to hear her out.

In a time when the dominant language is shaped by bombs and wars, *On Reconciliation* offers a new language for imagining the future of Israelis and Palestinians, one grounded in political imagination, recognition, and equality. Israelis and Palestinians, like many people living in conflict zones around the world, are often convinced that their conflict is uniquely unsolvable, that their enemies are evil in ways never experienced in history, and that the other side could never accept a solution. Yet while every conflict has its own unique elements, many of the underlying dynamics, and the principles needed for resolution, remain similar.

Like Maya, I also spent time in Rwanda and South Africa, and I was moved to tears many times while there. I left both countries with a renewed belief that Israelis and Palestinians have much to learn from other conflicts. Rwanda experienced one of the most horrific genocides in history: one million people were killed in just three months. The level of dehumanization and oppression in South Africa is beyond what most people in the world can imagine. And yet, both societies found ways to pursue reconciliation, break the cycle of violence, and shape a new reality. It is by no means a perfect reality in either country, but it has saved lives and created a path toward a better future.

I do not expect Palestinians or Israelis to be enthusiastic about the painful sacrifices that peacemaking requires. Many Palestinians will ask: How can we move toward reconciliation without punishing the enforcers and architects of the occupation? Doesn't justice mean holding accountable those who committed crimes?

While working in Northern Ireland, I met Alan McBride, whose wife was killed in an IRA terrorist attack. When I asked him why he campaigned for the "Yes" vote that ultimately led to the release of his wife's killer from prison, he told me that the future of his daughter was more important to him than revenge.

He told me how he cried the first time he saw the killer in a supermarket in his neighborhood. I know from my own life that his grief and pain will never disappear. Maya doesn't argue that peace will erase the trauma and pain we have experienced for decades. Rather, with stories from Rwanda and South Africa, she shows us that the pain of making peace is worth bearing because the alternative is endless death and destruction.

On Reconciliation makes the argument that since we are destined to live together, we must find a way to share the land. We must reject the logic of war and destruction, and begin imagining a different future, one in which our children no longer fear the sound of sirens or exploding missiles, the roar of airplanes dropping bombs, the pounding of soldiers at the door in the middle of the night, or the phone call informing us of yet another victim in our family.

The logic of peace and reconciliation is rooted in this hope for a better future. It is rooted in our love for our children and in our refusal to allow our failures to create more graveyards for the victims of war and violence. As Maya puts it, we have no alternative. The only question is how many lives will be lost and how much more destruction we will endure before we understand that reconciliation is the only path out of the current situation. Yes, we've had peace negotiations fail, but the failure of previous negotiations should not lead us to surrender hope. We have witnessed countless failed wars and endless escalations that have brought neither security nor freedom. Why do we give war unlimited chances, yet fear taking a leap of faith toward a peace agreement that could transform our discourse and our future? No peace agreement will ever be perfect. Maya is not imagining a utopia, because no such place exists.

Reconciliation is an ongoing process, one that we will continue working toward throughout our lives. Over time, we will grow into it and become better at it. I remember walking through the streets of Kigali late at night to get ice cream, feeling completely safe, and meeting young people in Rwanda pursuing their dreams without fear, and thinking how much has changed! I remember speaking with black artists in South Africa and hearing about their aspirations. These experiences helped me imagine a world in which our future can look like theirs. That is why this book is so important: it brings these experiences to our peoples so that we, too, can imagine, dream, and build a different future.

I have worked in more than sixty countries around the world, and I have come to the same conclusion that Maya has highlighted in *On Reconciliation*. It is essential for us to draw upon local traditions, local knowledge, and indigenous peacebuilding practices. Maya shows how Rwanda's gacaca community reconciliation model succeeded far better than any imported Western peacebuilding framework could have. Palestinians and Israelis must also bring our own cultural knowledge and traditions of peacemaking into this process. Reconciliation is not a foreign concept to either Palestinians or Israelis, but it must be adapted to our own cultures to succeed.

Finally, *On Reconciliation* is a hopeful book – a book that will expand your imagination of what is possible and challenge you to reevaluate your assumptions about conflict and peace. It is personal, informative, truthful, inspiring, and, most importantly, deeply challenging. It presents a vision that all of us can become part of, if we allow our minds and hearts to imagine, to dream, and to act upon that dream.

Translator's Note

Todd Hasak-Lowy

IN THE PERIOD immediately following the attacks of October 7, 2023, it became common in Israel for people to say that they had "sobered up." At long last they were able to see clearly who stood on the other side of the conflict. Talk of peace and coexistence, in the opinion of these recently sober Israelis, was the talk of a deluded, dangerous idealism. There was only one language the Palestinians understood: force.

And so Israeli sobriety after October Seventh paved the way for a military campaign of unprecedented brutality, a campaign that, as of this writing, continues, and continues expanding in scope.

Make no mistake: *On Reconciliation* is, in its way, an extremely idealistic book, since it asks us to imagine a different, better future, a future in which reconciliation replaces conflict. But this book is also one of the most sober, and sobering, books I've read in some time. Yes, Maya Savir asks us to consider taking the leap into reconciliation. But not because some utopia awaits on the other side.

These pages, again and again, make it clear that whatever form Israeli-Palestinian reconciliation will take, the process will be deeply imperfect and indescribably painful. It will not be synonymous with justice. It will not erase trauma. It will not undo the past. All it will do – and this "all" must be enough – is make possible a future that is different than our terrible present. The promise of reconciliation is that our children, or at least our children's children, can live lives not dominated by conflict.

The unwavering truth at the center of *On Reconciliation* is that Israelis and Palestinians are destined to live together. The only question is how. The answer, for decades, has been conflict. *On Reconciliation* lucidly and persuasively lays out the alternative. The cases of South Africa and Rwanda are presented not as paragons of reconciliation; rather, they are explored as instances in which terribly violent societies have found a way to embrace coexistence and reject conflict. Their processes are flawed, but they have nonetheless made possible better futures.

All of us are destined to live together. In Israel, Palestine, England, the United States, everywhere. The polarized atmosphere of our current reality brings with it fantasies of domination and erasure. But that is the stuff of delusion. The time has come for all of us to sober up and embrace reconciliation, not because it's perfect but because it is the best path forward.

Prologue

IF YOU'VE PICKED UP THIS BOOK, I'm guessing that you're sick of conflict. There's a part of you – so small, skeptical, and fragile it often seems out of reach – that believes it's possible to end conflict.

Or perhaps the opposite is true.

You picked up this book because you used to believe it is possible to end conflict, including the Israeli-Palestinian conflict, but this belief has been shaken. You're heartbroken at having lost hope, but you no longer see a solution.

Most people where I live – Jews and Palestinians alike – identify with one of these positions, and sometimes alternate between them.

WHAT RELEVANCE could reconciliation possibly have in this moment? I write these words at the lowest point in the history of the Israeli-Palestinian conflict, lower even than the Dead Sea, the lowest spot on earth. It seems today that reconciliation and conflict (along with its end point, war) are parallel universes where not only the language is different, but the logic itself.

Both conflict and reconciliation are manifestations of humanity, just as day and night are manifestations of the ever-changing interactions between the exact same celestial bodies.

Therefore, though intuitively it may seem impossible, even at the height of conflict, reconciliation continues to exist as a very real possibility. The same societies that produced conflict can realign to produce reconciliation, much as the shifting positions of the earth, moon, and sun can turn night into day.

So there is no better time to consider, explore, and demand reconciliation. There is no better time to recall what is so easy to forget when you're trapped in a conflict that seems to have no solution:

All conflicts end.

It's in their nature. Even the very worst of wars – world wars and genocides – are proof of this.

The only question is how much more time and how many more lives will be lost before this end arrives.

Another truth is hidden inside that first truth: we are less rigid and closed up than we think. Humans are capable of change and societies are as well.

LIVING IN CONFLICT means a life where loss, pain, and helplessness are normalized. Indeed, they are normalized to such an extent that normal things – growth, beauty, self-fulfillment – appear strange.

Living in conflict means taking part in, and in fact being part of, a relationship that is at once symbiotic and sick.

Reconciliation transforms this relationship. Reconciliation heals it.

Conflict minimizes a person's freedom, much as poverty does. In fact, it prevents a person from realizing their full potential. It's impossible to overstate how much of a person's physical, emotional, and moral resources are consumed by living in conflict. A life free of conflict is a basic right of every human.[1]

Conflict's driving forces, its logic, penetrate every layer of life.

It is impossible to wage war without disregarding, to one extent or another, the suffering of those you're fighting against, and it is impossible to disregard this other without also disregarding parts of yourself, including aspects of your own suffering, namely, all that you must sacrifice in order to continue living in conflict.

1 The Universal Declaration of Human Rights, Article 3: "The right to life, liberty and security of person."

This means it is impossible to inflict suffering on another without inflicting suffering on yourself, without diminishing your own humanity.

Striving to end conflict means holding tight to your humanity, refusing to give up on it, refusing to give up on ourselves.

BUT IT IS VERY, VERY DIFFICULT to see these truths when you're trapped in conflict.

When you're ill, it's hard to think about anything but your physical suffering. When you're heartbroken, it's hard to feel anything but your heartbreak. It's even hard to imagine a situation in which your heart heals and opens up again.

Living in conflict is much the same, as it narrows your view of what exists and what is possible.

Yet you can enlarge your view of what is possible by turning your attention to other conflicts that ended with and through reconciliation. Learning about these cases will remind you of what is so easily forgotten when you're surrounded only by indescribable pain, retaliation, and suffering, and it seems that there's nothing on the horizon but more pain, more retaliation, and more indescribable suffering.

These other, very recent histories show that you are neither foolish nor naive to hope and work for a better future, a future of reconciliation, equality, safety, and, yes, even peace.

This book lays out a path for recovery from conflict. It shows that a different future is possible, and it offers you the tools for reaching it.

IN FEBRUARY 2014, I visited South Africa, where black and white citizens went through a reconciliation process after nearly fifty years of racist and oppressive rule by the white minority over the black majority. In October of that same year, I went to Rwanda, where the Hutu and Tutsi (the two ethnic groups that comprise most of the country's population) reconciled after members of the Hutu rose up against members of the Tutsi and perpetrated a genocide against them.

Between these two visits, the Israeli summer blazed.

And a war, another one, was set off between Israel and Gaza. My use of passive voice does not reflect a fatalistic view that sees war, this war or any other, as a decree from on high. It reflects, perhaps, the feeling of helplessness that overwhelmed me in witnessing what seemed like a rerun of the same tragedy, with the actors yet again performing their roles with astonishing obedience. This obedience may also be a function of the fact that our consciousness is so rigid, so constricted that we're unaware we're obeying anything at all, and are thus unable to imagine a different possibility, one in which we don't bleed. More on this later.

I came to Africa because of food, or more precisely, the lack thereof. My trips to South Africa, Rwanda, Ethiopia, Kenya, Uganda, and the Democratic Republic of Congo were part of my job as executive director of JustSpirulina, a Tel Aviv–based NGO that focused on the treatment and prevention of malnutrition. In this humanitarian initiative, high school students from the Herzliya Hebrew Gymnasium in Tel Aviv worked in partnership with underprivileged communities, sharing their know-how in cultivating spirulina, an extraordinarily nutritious species of microalgae. The idea was that after acquiring this knowledge, each community would pass it on to another, creating a chain of solidarity and nutrition. In South Africa and Rwanda, knowledge flowed in both directions: we offered agricultural and technological expertise while seeking to learn from their experiences with the process of reconciliation. It was important for me to emphasize this reciprocity at the time. Not out of any pretension that I could break the mold of the sad, shameful, and deeply rooted power relations between savior and victim all on my own (despite my desire to do so). I merely hoped to signal the possibility of a different balance of power.

As I return to this book for its translation and write the final chapter, "Reconciliation After October Seventh," I am painfully and shamefully aware that a lack of food – a famine crafted by my government – is spreading in Gaza, just over an hour's drive from my home. In the visuals pouring in from Gaza I recognize the swollen bellies of children suffering from kwashiorkor, a severe form of malnutrition. I recognize their eyes and their somewhat detached gaze, signaling that these children's departure from life may have begun. In conversations with friends and colleagues in Gaza I hear descriptions that evoke some of the more painful situations I encountered in Africa: at some point, malnourished children lose their appetite. Expressionless, they look at whatever meager food is handed to them as if it has nothing to do with them. In the face of such horrifying, unjustifiable reality, I am again compelled to act to bring it to an end, and to search for the path to reconciliation.

I always carry a notebook with me. You never know when an idea will flicker or a fragment will surface that demands a metaphor capable of freeing it from the limitations of its physical context. In the flood of experiences during my visits to Africa, it seemed my pen almost never left the page. Work-related matters intermixed with my impressions from discussions with people. Because I was in a constant writing position, I felt as if I were a pupil seated before my conversation partners.

During my decade of work on this initiative, I interacted with students and teachers, janitors and principals, farmers and agronomists, researchers and scholars, representatives of local organizations and government officials. But most of the conversations – the backbone of this book – were conducted during trips to help build infrastructure and conduct training for spirulina cultivation in South Africa (February 2014) and in Rwanda (October 2014 and September 2015). These conversations took place while building greenhouses and during training sessions, on the sidelines of work meetings, while walking or driving on roads, and in shared living quarters. I'm still in touch with many of the people I met and worked with back then.

In this book, these people will be identified by the initial of their first name only. Some of them live in a society where they cannot freely express themselves. As I would like the reader to think of them the same as the others, I refer to everyone in the same manner.

Operating within an overwhelming and taxing reality with the aim of changing something about it – in this case, the issue that brought me there, nutrition – demanded a sustained effort that is generally unknown to someone who takes their daily survival for granted. Simply put, the fantasy of being a "fly on the wall" vanished, leaving behind only a longing for those moments of grace that would allow me to mentally step back, moments of observation and contemplation. I operated as a camera and tape recorder, jotting down fragments of descriptions, conversations, and experiences, flashes of thoughts and insights, without lingering on any of them, so they wouldn't dissolve into this intensive reality filled with contradictions. The enormous, almost illogical amount of events squeezed into a short timeframe bestowed a dream-like quality onto what was actually a very tangible, earthy reality, in the face of which I could do nothing but note this and press on.

BACK IN TEL AVIV, with the 2014 war ongoing, my eight-year-old son and I were returning from day camp one afternoon. I calculated our steps from one building to the next, planning where to run if the sirens sounded.

"How was camp today?" I asked, as usual.

"Fun," he answered, also as usual, and added: "We played IDF against Hamas." Heartrendingly nonchalant, unintentionally ironic, he recounted how some of the children were the Israel Defense Forces and others were Hamas. They threw things at each other, took cover, and simulated the sounds of sirens and explosions with their voices.

"And who won?" I asked.

"No one," he replied simply. "After a while we got tired," he explained, "so we stopped."

In war, as in summer camp, at some point the sides get tired and stop – even though when the fighting is over, the reality that (ostensibly) led to the war remains unchanged.

Only the amount of sorrow in the world has increased.

IN THIS BOOK, as in my previous books, I write in an effort to understand. Translating reality into text is my primary way of contending with reality. For as long as I can remember, I've never really understood something until I found the words to describe it. And in this book, as in my other books, I write in order to challenge reality. In writing, freedom is infinite, and it's possible to disrupt what seems to be immutable.

However, there was an additional motive for writing this book, one engendered by a sense of distress, along with an awareness of something else. A thick and sticky distress grew from the realization that despite my active affiliation with the Left, my very existence in Israel makes me part of the conflict, part of the system that sustains it, one of those who must be held accountable and bear responsibility for it. As for the awareness, this I can't prove – as it is based on moral, historical, and perhaps also literary intuition – but nevertheless I am as certain about it as I can be about anything: groups aspire toward self-determination and equality, and over time they ultimately realize these things; oppressive regimes are destined to disappear, and religious psychoses run out of steam. A day will come when we, our children, our grandchildren, or their children will look back on the conflict we're living in today as a thing of the past. The only question is how much time will pass and how much blood will be spilled in the meantime. And at that future moment, those who lived through the conflict will ask themselves – and will be asked – what their moral stance was, and whether they even had one, and if they did anything to change their reality.

My encounters with South Africa and Rwanda, two societies that had undergone reconciliation processes, intensified my awareness of the folly of the conflicted existence that contains our lives. It left me stammering and bewildered, and brought me to write this book, which is a collection of my personal impressions and those of the people I met there who are still contending with the very personal challenges that reconciliation has posed and continues to pose. Through observation, reflection, and conversation, I seek to learn the meaning of reconciliation, identify its components, and understand which are essential to its actualization. By peeling away what is nonessential, I aim to isolate the characteristics that are common to the very dissimilar societies of South Africa and Rwanda, but which are lacking in Israeli society. Perhaps – hopefully – they'll offer us a clue.

In the final chapter, "Reconciliation After October Seventh," I revisit these notions and ask the terrifying and obvious question: Is reconciliation possible after everything that's happened since October Seventh?

1

A Consciousness Cast in Conflict

WHEN WE THINK OF A CHILD who has been abused, we take certain things for granted. It is obvious to us, for example, that such a child will have difficulty thinking of an adult in terms of protection and that he might, when he himself is an adult, reproduce the same patterns with his own children. When we think of a battered woman, we assume that this woman understands the relationship with her partner in terms of reward and punishment and that she might, to one extent or another, feel that she deserves the treatment she receives. When we think of a person who grew up and lives in a nondemocratic society, we assume that this person will be less inclined to think independently and critically, and that he also tends to accept outrageous realities as a matter of necessity.

Experience and research tell us what common sense knows: harsh realities constrict, narrow, and cloud consciousness.

And yet we are slow to apply this understanding to those who were born, raised, and shaped in a society steeped in conflict. We are slow to apply this understanding to ourselves. Perhaps because, like an abused child, a battered woman, or someone living under a dictatorial regime, we too are imprisoned in the limits of our constricted, narrowed, and clouded consciousness, to the point that we cannot grasp that such is our situation.

So what does a consciousness cast in conflict look like, and what does this mean for our ability to perceive our situation and the possibility of changing it? Common sense suggests, at least to some extent, that the form of our consciousness reflects the conflictual reality of which we are but a part. Conflicts differ in their content: they can be religious, racial, territorial, national, or a combination. However, all conflicts have formal traits in common: a *separation* between "us" and "them"; an *object* toward which both sides aspire; and an explicit or implicit assumption that the only possible relationship between one of the parties and the object is that of *exclusion*. These forms are seared into a consciousness that is a product of conflict. They become the patterns through which reality is perceived.

P is a science teacher at a boarding school in Cape Town, South Africa. During the ten days I stayed at the boarding school, I had the opportunity to see him teaching his students, listening to them and advising them. On the margins of the days, we talked about his dream of making art, the obstacles reality places before that dream, and his sense of mission as an educator. He hoped to rise above the curriculum's rigid demands and pass on to his students some of what he learned from a dedicated professor, a man who taught him how to think beyond the tyranny of those thought patterns he had absorbed from his environment. Even when he reached adulthood and became an activist in the fight for equal rights and a member of the African National Congress's teachers' union, he found it difficult to think outside the racial categories on which he had been raised. "Whites were better than colored people and colored people were better than black people. That's how it was. Everyone knew it. I don't think my parents ever asked themselves if that's how things *needed* to be, and I accepted this division as something natural. We were colored, this defined us, and that was that. Even as we opposed discrimination, we thought within this division."

To think *within* such a division means that obedience has seeped into the patterns dictated by the conflict – into thinking, neutralizing the mind's most precious asset: its independence. Is this not horrific?

This, however horrific, is not an exhaustive description of a consciousness produced by conflict. After all, this describes a situation in which *some* thinking, however weakened, still occurs about something that can be *seen*, in this case the existence of black, colored, and white people in the country. And this thinking includes the common-sense assumption that some kind of relationship exists between them. But – and this is so embarrassing to recognize in retrospect! – there is much we can't even pretend to think about, because our compliance with these conflict-produced patterns won't let us. At the very least, such patterns hinder our effort to see things fully. We don't see things we don't want to see, because seeing them would completely undermine the way we perceive ourselves and the group to which we belong: family, society, country. In other words, a consciousness produced by conflict protects itself from reality and functions as a gatekeeper in the face of it. And if some fragment of that which is not to be seen slips through, it exists in our consciousness free from that larger "forbidden" and "dangerous" context. And so we treat that fragment as a separate, independent, and random particle, not as part of some bigger, significant phenomenon that deserves our attention.

S, a slender, elegant woman, spoke with me about this acquired blindness. She's in her fifties and works as a teacher and social activist with the poor black population, one plagued by drugs, alcohol, and crime, in the streets of Cape Town, South Africa. With her well-kept blonde bob, pencil skirts, and stiletto heels, she looks like a character who has accidentally found herself placed inside the wrong painting. In all of my conversations with her, I found myself looking for this artist, who has since left the scene, in order to ask him: "Excuse me, but didn't you confuse this?" However, as she saw it, the one who placed her in this painting was God, who in his goodness gave her the opportunity to atone – in her life, in her deeds, in every moment – for the injustices committed by white people during the apartheid years. More precisely, God gave her the opportunity to atone not only for what other white people did in her name, because she was white, but also for the fact that she was entirely ignorant about all this. Because she could have known, had she made the effort.

"You see," she said to me with her big, watery blue eyes, sometimes moved to tears, though it was clear she was trying to emphasize that she's not the victim in her stories. "You see, I didn't know! I grew up on a farm in the Limpopo region, near the border with Zimbabwe. It's a really wild area, where lions roam, so people live on very large, well-protected farms. My father was a lovely man, a man of honesty and faith, and he treated the blacks who lived with us on the farm very well. Their children studied with us, with my brother and me, and with the private tutors who came to the farm. We didn't go to school. Our whole lives were there. And we played together, the children of the black workers and us, our whole childhood we were together. I didn't even know there was apartheid. I mean," she qualifies, "I knew that beyond our farm, which was really something of a bubble, blacks weren't treated as well as whites. But I didn't *really* know. I didn't know *how much worse*. I think my father tried to protect us," she said, tearing up yet again, "I think he didn't want us to know that there was such evil in the world. But when I grew up and went to university, I was shocked. One day a policeman came up to me and told me that I was walking on the wrong street, meaning a street designated for blacks. He was very polite and kind and spoke to me as if I had made a simple mistake and he was just alerting me to my mistake, for my own good, so that I could quickly return to the street for whites. He was right that I didn't know about such segregation, and he was right that I was walking there by mistake, but the moment I discovered my mistake, my life changed."

It's sad, even a little insulting, to see the imprint conflict makes on a consciousness, since we then must recognize that, to one degree or another, all of us are limited by these patterns. Most of us – even when trying to be "enlightened" – think with an "us" and "them" dichotomy. Most of us see the very heart of the conflict in the piece of land so deeply coveted by both "us" and "them," and most of us struggle to imagine a situation in which "us" and "them" exist as equals on that same piece of land. Anything that doesn't conform to these thought patterns is doomed – as in S's case – to remain outside the boundaries of consciousness or to enter its gates only after being transformed beyond recognition.

But it seems to me that it is precisely these things – these fragments of human existence and this denied reality – that should interest us. Not only do they embody the price we pay, they also represent the end of a thread leading to a reality different from the one in which we currently bleed. Yet the end of this thread leads to something that lies beyond our consciousness, and there's the rub: our attempt to grasp it is in fact an attempt to grasp something unknown, analogous perhaps to the effort required to use a word that is "on the tip of one's tongue" or to hold on to a fragment of a dream in order to reconstruct it.

Although it is difficult to put one's finger on the exact nature of those things that are doomed to transform or disappear into an oblivion beyond our awareness, it seems possible to characterize them as threatening the "order," those rigid, opaque distinctions that have shaped the landscape of our consciousness. The humanity, uniqueness, and singularity of a private individual are obscured and sometimes erased completely by a consciousness shaped through conflict. The individual is left only with the characteristics of his "group," which gives these things greater weight. The process works in both directions: a person has difficulty seeing the other, his "enemy," and at the same time, in order to do this, he denies those humane, unique, and singular parts of himself.

But back to us Israelis, and to a little story that perhaps sums up the cognitive prison we live in. R, a senior surgeon and a lifelong peace and human rights activist, told me the following story with a combination of irony, self-deprecation, and perhaps even a little relief that stems from the realization that the conflict has left its mark on him, too, and in such a way as to bring him closer to those he is trying to convince that coexistence in this place is actually possible.

"A fifteen-year-old boy came to the hospital seriously wounded," he said. "He was shot by the IDF while throwing stones in Nablus. Hello, I said to him, I'm your doctor. Where does it hurt? The boy wouldn't say a thing. His lips were pressed together, his pale face dotted with two jet-black eyes that burned with a fierce hatred. I could see all the world's hatred in them. Again I told him that I was his doctor and that I wanted to help him. Through clenched lips, the boy hissed just one word: jihad. I smiled at him and again asked what hurt. And again, the boy said only one word: jihad. The surgery was difficult and complicated and lasted all through the night." R continued to speak in the literary Hebrew of someone not born into the language but who nevertheless learned its subtleties and nuances. A kind of gratitude for this fluency, achieved with great effort, could be heard in his words. "The boy was saved." He let out a loud sigh, as if experiencing the relief all over again. "That morning, as I left the operating room, I met the boy's father, also a doctor. Unlike his son, he spoke English. He held out his hand to me. 'Professor, I will forever be grateful to you for saving my son's life.' We shook hands firmly and warmly. 'Your son is rather stubborn,' I said, telling him how his son didn't want to talk to us and would only say 'jihad' over and over again, and in fact refused to cooperate with us. The father thanked me again, and again said he owed me his life, but then he added: 'Professor, I am Ahmed and my son . . . his name is Jihad.' Look how impossible it is to escape from this," R said to me. "I, who define myself as a humanist and like to believe that all people are equal in my eyes, I fell into a stereotypical trap and heard what I expected to hear from a boy throwing stones at soldiers. That determined my interpretation, even though it turns out that Jihad has been a common name in Islam long before it was appropriated by those calling for a holy war. It is the commandment to uphold the laws of Islam and spread the teachings of the Prophet Muhammad."

Perhaps the hardest part about all this is recognizing that a consciousness formed in conflict knows nothing else and therefore struggles to even imagine an alternative. Similar, perhaps, to the difficulty a person blind from birth has in imagining what the sky looks like. I recognize this in my children, who were born around the time of Yitzhak Rabin's assassination and in the years that followed, and in fact are not familiar with the feeling of hope. For the sake of accuracy and fairness, I should acknowledge that the years 1992–95 were full of hope for those who thought the Oslo Accords brought with them the possibility of peace, but full of anxiety for those who thought it was a recipe for disaster. Whatever the case, this was a period when the possibility of a different future still existed. My children and their contemporaries have never experienced life here as offering anything other than conflict, which is sometimes quieter and sometimes deafening. They have never tasted, smelled, or felt hope. All they have is what has been passed down to them through stories. So how can they aspire to hope? How can they change their fate?

Change is hard. It seems to me that the human capacity to change is born in moments when a person is given the opportunity to imagine themselves or their reality differently. Such moments tend to be rare and fleeting, but they provide a glimpse into what is typically unseen and perhaps even unimagined. Sometimes it's not even a glimpse, but only a vague feeling – of tenderness, of comfort, of breathing freely. However, once experienced, this sliver of insight exists, it's tangible, and one can – if one so chooses – attempt to recreate it and perhaps expand it to other realms of existence.

In this, I believe, lies the value of looking outward, of searching for such moments with those who have succeeded in thinking outside of the patterns that conflict creates, in imagining for themselves another life, one in which conflict is not simply a given.

2

The Uniqueness of a Conflict

BEFORE WE GO ANY FURTHER with other cases, perhaps it's worthwhile to take a moment to ask whether there is indeed any basis for comparing the Israeli-Palestinian conflict to the conflicts of South Africa and Rwanda, and then (because the answer is yes, there is), to take another moment to ponder the difficulties that such comparisons raise.

After all, these aren't simple comparisons. South Africa, Israel, Rwanda: it sometimes seems that these aren't just wildly different places, but phenomena that belong to altogether separate categories. So, it's foolish to try to connect them – it would be like attempting to build a triangle from an apple, a giraffe, and a whistle, and not simply three sticks.

It's difficult, nearly impossible, to avoid falling into clichés when trying to describe the breadth and depth of the differences between these three countries. Colors that come from a different palette; aromas that powerfully act on the olfactory receptors, which seem to be created ad hoc because the ones that exist aren't sufficient for smelling everything there is to smell; and a rhythm which is unaffected by human action. It's a given, like a companion of equal status, and no one tries to catch up with it or slow it down, to own it or to deny it. "You, the Europeans (a common term for foreigners, even when they're not Europeans), have an issue with time," J told me in Rwanda when we were trying to plan together the next steps of our project. "You attach it to things that aren't at all *connected* to it, and so you allow it to take control of them," he explained, and then he shared a joke the locals like to tell among themselves: A man, a European, came to Africa and did something bad, so they put him in prison. At mealtime, they served noodles, but the man didn't understand that they would eventually bring sauce too. He thought that if they don't come *at the same time*, they are no longer together. And so he ate bland noodles.

Even the African sky seems different, almost within reach, as if the familiar boundaries between heaven and earth have been blurred. It is also a different way of thinking that is hard to grasp and conceptualize, because when we attempt to do this, we are equipped only with the tools that are the product of our way of thinking. The philosopher Ludwig Wittgenstein noted that if you ask a person how much two plus two is, and they answer five, it would be a mistake. But if they answer ninety-seven, it would not be a mistake. The person you're speaking with operates within a completely different logic than yours.

This disparity is intrinsic to what makes it difficult to compare the conflicts and raises the question of whether it is possible, for me in this case, to say anything significant about South Africa and Rwanda based on my limited knowledge; whether it is possible to learn about a place or person from an external perspective, from observation and listening, and not from the perspective of someone who is part of the place; and, no less than this, whether it is possible to express those insights that are within reach without falling into gross generalizations and embarrassing clichés.

I think that despite the difficulty, it is possible to say something significant. I also think it is worthwhile to do this, or at least to try to do this, but only provided that we place a caveat before every such statement, a sort of signpost of humility that declares: I'm offering these insights of mine with caution, fully aware of their limitations, and I present them here very gingerly as my own personal interpretation.

Another difficulty that accompanies my effort to compare the conflicts is linguistic, and has to do not with the question of the legitimacy of saying something significant, but the ability to do this in words. When I landed for the first time in Kigali and stood in the slow-moving line at passport control, I was surprised by a pungently sweet aroma that seemed completely out of place, an aroma with which I was intimately familiar, though I couldn't place it. It took me another moment before connecting the smell to a young jasmine plant in a small flowerpot; the man in front of me in line was holding the flowerpot in his hand. The delicate white petals brought me back through the fragrant gate formed by the jasmine that climbed and twined up the façade of my childhood home in Jerusalem. Perhaps the man with the plant sensed the excitement rippling through me, or perhaps he simply was seeking a human connection in a place that was also foreign to him. He waited for me to take my eyes off the flower and, after making eye contact, said: "I'm here to visit a friend. I want to tell him about my home in Tunisia. I want him to understand where I come from, and how can I do that?" He shrugged his shoulders. "So I'm bringing this flower for him to smell." Sometimes a flower can reach a place that words can only strive toward.

My interest in the linguistic aspects of reconciliation grew from my struggle to find the right words during my encounters with South Africa and Rwanda. This struggle for words was more acute than the one I regularly experience when writing (like anyone who writes, I suppose), and intensified whenever I attempted to use the same concepts to describe these realities that are so different from one another. "English is an unfit medium for the truth of South Africa," the South African author J. M. Coetzee writes in his novel *Disgrace*. In my case, I felt that my words were not only unfit to describe Africa; they became diluted and lost their meaning when applied there. And when I began using them again to describe the reality of my life, I found they had become feeble. They no longer did the job.

While in South Africa, I stayed together with my coworkers at a boarding school in Cape Town, where we worked. The teenagers from Tel Aviv shared rooms with the teenagers studying at the school. Some of them formed connections that continued via social media in the following years. The boys and girls learning at the school ranged in age from fifteen to eighteen and came from all parts of the country. They were identified as having high academic potential; all were from challenging backgrounds.

"Challenging background" – here's a term that needs to be stretched thin, stretched until nothing is left of it, before it can be applied to both those particular instances of "challenging background" that we're familiar with from our own reality and the particular instances of such children at this boarding school. It's like using the term "sickness" to describe both the common cold and cancer. Between dinner at 5 p.m. (a hot but meager meal, without any fresh fruit or vegetables) and breakfast the next day at 7 a.m., the only ones who eat are those whose families are able to send them back with snacks after they visit their homes (once every three weeks for those who can afford the trip; others visit home once every three months). When the teenagers from Tel Aviv discovered this, they made a habit of buying cakes and candy at the supermarket and sharing them with their roommates at small nocturnal parties, with music playing from the speakers of their cell phones.

One evening, a girl from another dorm room walked into the room where some other girls, both South African and Israeli, were staying. Perhaps she was drawn by the scent of food, perhaps by the rustling of bags, or maybe she just happened to be passing by. "She stood near the entrance and told us she was hungry," the girls recounted the next morning. "We shared what we had, but she won't be able to eat everything," they added, confused and embarrassed. "She doesn't have teeth . . . at all . . . she has no teeth." P and Z, the school's science teachers, nodded sadly when I asked them if they knew which girl this was. P and

Z are husband and wife. They live at the boarding school and, in the absence of parents, doctors, and counselors, fill these roles for the boarding school kids. "Yes, but she's not the only one. Many poor families cannot take care of their children's teeth," they explained. "When there's a cavity, they simply have the tooth pulled out. And if it's a baby tooth and it's pulled out too early, the adult tooth never grows in." It's hard to fathom this, but in the world in which we live, there's a sixteen-year-old girl who studies from 8 a.m. to 9 p.m., with only a one-hour break. Every day. Thanks to the opportunity given to her at the boarding school, perhaps she will succeed in lifting herself out of poverty. Perhaps not. In the meantime, she's hungry and has no teeth.

The combination of "child" and a possessive pronoun – "my child," "her child," "his child" – appears frequently in regular discourse. It signifies something factual and establishes some order in our society; such expressions are not seen as stirring up ambivalent feelings. As parents, the first-person form – "my son," "our daughter" – arouses pleasant, comforting associations, and pride. However, when encountering a hungry child – in Africa, and a decade later, to my endless shame, in the visuals from Gaza – I find that the glue binding this attachment dissolves and the identity of the person claiming possession diminishes. A hungry child cannot belong to one particular person or set of parents. A hungry child belongs to everyone, to all of humanity. But this runs contrary to our patterns of thinking, which emphasize separateness and otherness, and thus renders the categories of "my child," "her child," and "his child" meaningless. In post-genocide Rwanda, a large number of orphans roamed the streets and fields. In many cases, these terrified and starving children were taken into homes by people who didn't know them and didn't know "whose" children they were. They took care of them and raised them because they were "everyone's" children.

Despite its limitations, language – in particular, linguistic differences among cultures – carries substantial power. As a signifier of its speakers, of their culture and character, language can detect conflict and direct us toward aspects of conflict that we've already lost sight of. In the same way, it can serve as a detector of reconciliation, directing us toward aspects of it that can be found in South Africa and Rwanda, but are missing in Israel and Palestine.

I'll start with what we can learn from dictionaries and definitions. The Hebrew word *piyus* and its English equivalent, *reconciliation*, belong to similar, but not overlapping, semantic fields. It seems unnecessary to elaborate on the similarity between these Hebrew and English words. However, the differences between them might offer a new angle for discussion. That is, even if we set aside for a moment the question of whether thought is a product of language, or language a product of thought, the connection between them is recognized by all, and it is reasonable to assume that the words we speak or do not speak reveal something about us.

First (and perhaps also second and third, because this discovery continues to stun me – and occasionally sends me to check again, to confirm that I didn't overlook an entry), *piyus* does not even appear as an entry in the Hebrew version of Wikipedia (unless we count the lineage of popes named Pius). In contrast, the "Reconciliation" page in the English version of Wikipedia offers a gateway to entries from different worlds: everything from accounting to Christian theology, as well as extensive entries on the Truth and Reconciliation Commission in South Africa and the process of coming to terms with the past in post–World War II Germany. This difference can be explained by the huge number of authors and readers contributing to and engaging with the English-language version of this body of knowledge (including many for whom English is not their only or primary language) versus the number of authors and readers of the Hebrew version, by the geographic distribution and great diversity of the former versus the latter, or even just by the enormous disparity between the number of entries in the English version (over five million) versus the number of entries in the Hebrew version (less than 200,000). However, this explanation ignores the fact that Wikipedia is a body of knowledge based on the wisdom and knowledge of the crowd, and presumably reflects its values too. And in Hebrew, as noted, there is no such entry. Not even an entry that describes it as something negative. The Hebrew terms for "conflict resolution" (in all its lexical variations) and "transitional justice" also do not appear in the Hebrew version of Wikipedia. Related entries like "Alternative Methods for Resolving Conflicts" and "Restorative Justice" appear, but are limited to the field of law.

Dictionaries, on the other hand, are not supposed to be influenced by the number of people who speak a language, and they include most of the words in a language at the time they are compiled. They represent, therefore, a significant part of the consciousness of those who speak the language. The differences between the semantic fields of the Hebrew word and the English word are interesting. The semantic field of *reconciliation* also includes the theoretical level, according to which different ideas and different facts can co-exist or be correct at the same time,[1] while *piyus* refers only to the concrete level.[2] It seems to me that this difference is of particular significance, because the concrete level of exiting from conflict is expressed in agreements between the sides, whereas reconciliation pertains to areas that are more difficult to quantify – narrative, emotions, personal experience, and justice – and these do not resonate in the Hebrew word *piyus*.

Similarly, reconciliation not only means coming to terms with a rival, but also entails an internal process of acceptance. This is significant because people in reconciling societies are required not only to come to terms with each other, but also

1 Merriam-Webster: The process of finding a way to make two different ideas, facts, etc., exist or be true at the same time.

2 Even-Shoshan Dictionary: Placation, mitigation of anger, solicitation of good things; peacemaking, mediation between rivals, elimination of the dispute. Other Hebrew dictionaries offer nearly identical definitions.

with demons that likely reside within themselves – their role in the conflict or avoidance of it, the relativity of their truth, and the personal price they paid during and after the conflict. *Reconciliation*, in contrast to *piyus*, also means demonstrating compatibility and creating harmony,[3] which brings us close to or into the realm of ideas – a realm too many Israelis avoid entirely, and in an idealistic manner unique to this subject. They either want a perfect reconciliation or none at all. More on that later.

Another difference is the element of entreating and placating that is present in *piyus* but not in *reconciliation*. It implies an asymmetrical balance of power where one side tries to get on the good side of the other, submitting to its power, presenting an offering. This is very significant because it represents an additional actor running wild in our field of play: dignity. On this point, there is overlap between the semantic field of *piyus* and that of *appeasement*.[4] Thus, it is not difficult to understand the aversion that this component of submissiveness brings to the word *piyus* for Israelis.

Turning our attention to language as it operates beyond the bounds of definitions and dictionaries sheds light on another characteristic of a society immersed in conflict: the corruption of language itself. The anguish of the conflict, the ambivalence toward it, and the guilt it engenders cause a society to undertake mental acrobatics whose psychological objective is clear: to alleviate anguish, deny ambivalence, and reduce guilt. In other words, the aim is to enable the speakers of the language to talk about something without really talking about it, without fully understanding it or placing it within an unpleasant context that might undermine their self-image or perception of reality. This is the kind of linguistic contortion one can find among families that bear a secret. Like an ostracized member of the family, the secret grows demanding and bitter. And even though it poisons

3 Oxford English Dictionary: harmonize, make compatible; show the compatibility of by argument or in practice.

4 Oxford English Dictionary: make calm or quiet, esp. conciliate (a potential aggressor) by making concessions.

the family members' individual and shared existence, it is only referred to in very general and noncommittal terms: the "thing" or the "incident," for example.

These mental acrobatics do not enhance the language, nor do they enrich it with nuance. Instead, they blur the connection (which is essential for the existence of language, any language) between the signifier and the signified. The linguistic products of such acrobatics are varied, and include an increased distance between the signifier and the signified; thus, we're able to speak, for example, about an "incident" in which a "wanted person" was "detained" without knowing what actually occurred. Was the wanted person arrested because he planned a terror attack? Or perhaps it was actually a fifteen-year-old from East Jerusalem whose Facebook post annoyed someone in the Shin Bet (Israel Security Agency) and soldiers burst into his home in the middle of the night to arrest him? Similarly, we can talk about the IDF "clearing" an area without imagining the way this is executed in reality, by demolishing homes, for instance, or by uprooting orchards that provide the sole livelihood for the people living there. This enables us, simply, not to know.

Another expression of the blurring of this connection can be found in the broadening of the domain signified by the signifier. The word thus becomes a sort of clearing house where many terms, not necessarily related, cohabitate – nuances be damned. So, a "terrorist" can be both someone who carries out a terror attack and, just the same, a ten-year-old boy who throws a stone at an IDF vehicle; and "incitement" can be a call to destroy Israel and can also express the desire to shed light – in a poem, for example – on the Palestinian catastrophe that took place alongside the creation of the State of Israel. This also operates in the opposite direction, with a narrowing of the domain that the signifier signifies. Thus, "child" will always be a Jewish child, while a Palestinian child is excluded from the domain of this signifier and is exiled to the domain of signifiers such as "terrorist" or "youth," which do not carry the risk of stirring compassion within us.

Another characteristic of the corruption of language concerns the confusion of domains, or more precisely, the use of words from one realm to speak about a different, unrelated realm. The use of the word "procedures" regarding an "incident" in which, let's say, innocent civilians were killed, should leave us sleepless because implied in the use of this word is that the investigation of this "incident" lies in the administrative, technical realm and not in the realm of morality. This confusion of realms allows us to draw the conclusion – only if there had been no deviation from those "procedures," of course– that there was no fault in this "incident." Another example can be found in the expression "neighbor procedure," which describes the IDF's use of civilians as human shields to get wanted persons out of a house. This expression is particularly ironic in the context of reconciliation because it is used to describe an action that has nothing in common with neighborly relations and actually belongs to the domain of warfare. Yet another example is the Regulation Law, designed by Israeli legislators intent on legalizing settlement outposts built on privately owned Palestinian land, where "regulation" is actually used to describe the retroactive legalization of unlawful actions.

A corrupted language is a sad language in which words betray their mission. They don't describe reality (external or internal); they blur it. They distance the speakers of the language from themselves instead of enabling greater intimacy with oneself.

Another linguistic feature that is interesting to consider is the domains in which a society applies the language – that is, the limits of discourse: what a society talks about and what it doesn't talk about. In South Africa and in Rwanda, despite the great difference between the societies and between their reconciliation processes, I found a discourse operating in a space centered around reconciliation, including the good it brought as well as its imperfections and the prices it exacted. In Israel, on the other hand, our discourse operates in a space that centers around what is lacking, the assertion that on the other side "there's no one to talk to." A difference of night and day. Something that exists versus something nonexistent. Presence versus absence. Something versus nothing.

Can something be created out of nothing? That's a question for the alchemists. Meanwhile, here in Israel, we've condemned ourselves to a rigid, restricted, self-perpetuating existence, an existence in which the impossibility of change necessarily limits everyone's degree of freedom, because a consciousness that fixates on what is absent is a consciousness of helplessness.

It's difficult to desire something that doesn't exist or that is unknown. And if, nonetheless, a desire of this sort awakens, it's usually a vague, faint desire, one that belongs more to the realm of questioning and searching than to the realm of action. Whatever the case, it's not a desire that can guide and enable a person to dig deep into their reality in order to find it.

Some explain this lack of options by claiming that the Israeli-Palestinian conflict, "our" conflict, is unique in its complexity. This assertion leads to another difficulty, as it touches on the ultimate question: Is it even possible to compare conflicts?

It's true that "our" conflict has been "blessed" with three factors, each sufficient all on its own to ignite and sustain a conflict: religion, territory, and nation. And in the background, like a soundtrack foreshadowing doom, lie assertions about colonialism, which are often raised in a sloppy fashion that fails to capture the complexity of the situation. Nevertheless, they highlight the different and even contradictory self-perceptions held by the two sides when it comes to who are the "foreign implants" in their land. In the conflict in South Africa, it was clear who was indigenous and who had emigrated to the state, and in Rwanda, two indigenous groups fought each other. In Israel and Palestine, however, there is a side that experienced the formation of the State of Israel as the climax of a colonial conquest that deprived it of its right to the land, and on the other hand, a side that claims historical and religious ties and a continual presence, however small, in the land. Whatever the case, the latter's attitude toward the local "other" contains more than a bit of the sense of superiority that characterizes colonialism everywhere.

It should be noted that religion, territory, and nation are not factors of equal weight. One need only ponder the religious aspect of the Israeli-Palestinian conflict for a moment to see that it's not a religious conflict in the simple sense, but rather a conflict in which religion functions as an emotional agent of conflict propaganda – in other words, religion is one of the tools used to justify it. Yet the three factors are significant in the conflict, and all three will play a role in any attempt to defuse it. It's hard to think of a more challenging entanglement. However, it's reasonable to argue that every conflict is unique and complex in its own way – to the extent that it isn't hard to understand how, once the conflict emerges full-blown, it becomes difficult, nearly impossible, for those immersed in it to imagine a solution.

Is it reasonable to claim that the issues underlying the protracted Israeli-Palestinian conflict are more difficult than those faced by other societies that were able to reconcile? That the injustices committed in our region are more appalling than those committed elsewhere?

In order to answer those questions, we'll need to look at those other conflicts, our competitors for the coveted title of being the "most" difficult, complex, bloody, cruel, and so on.

In South Africa, a white minority ruled over a black majority for nearly half a century. The apartheid ("separation" in Afrikaans[5]) regime dictated race-based population registration

5 The language of the Afrikaners (the descendants of Dutch settlers who arrived in the country in the seventeenth century), who comprised a majority of the white population. (The white population also included the descendants of British settlers who arrived later. Over the years, the two white groups fought each other for control of the country.) Afrikaans was the language most identified with the apartheid regime, in part due to efforts to impose it on the nonwhite population by making Afrikaans the language of instruction in schools, including those attended by nonwhite students.

(order was absolutely vital, after all, so each person had to be classified as black, white, or colored); a practice of complete racial separation, including in residential areas (nonwhite people, in fact, were completely banned from living in the cities), in education, in transportation, and in health services; restrictive legislation on property, employment, interracial marriage and sexual relations, movement, politics (for nonwhite citizens, political organization was essentially prohibited and the right to vote and be elected was denied); and of course, severe means of punishment intended to sustain the regime, including widespread arrests and incarceration of black leaders for many years, brutal policing, and the use of live gunfire to disperse demonstrations by organizations opposed to the regime, which were labeled "terrorist" organizations.

All of this was done, as noted, in accordance with the law, since the reins were entirely in white hands. They were the ones who drafted the laws in a way that justified even the worst injustices. Martin Luther King Jr. wrote about the connection between law and morality: "We should never forget that everything Adolf Hitler did in Germany was 'legal' and everything the Hungarian freedom fighters did in Hungary was 'illegal.' It was 'illegal' to aid and comfort a Jew in Hitler's Germany. Even so, I am sure that, had I lived in Germany at the time, I would have aided and comforted my Jewish brothers."[6] In order to understand the depth of exploitation and subjugation, it's important to add to the portrait of South Africa its non-unique hue, the same hue that painted the entire continent: colonialism. The country's racist regime was an addition to the colonialism that stained Africa, destroyed its social fabric, and excluded nonwhite people from the economic control of their countries, including the management of their natural resources.

Here it is in everyday terms: A child is born in South Africa during the years of apartheid. To his misfortune, he is black. This means that he grows up on the outskirts of a city, in one

6 "Letter from Birmingham Jail." April 16, 1963.

of the ghettos to which the black population was banished in order to "purify" the cities of their unpleasant presence, which sheds light precisely on what the white population would prefer not to see, their own reflection included. In this ghetto, the township, he lives in a small home, typically built of tin and plywood. Sometimes there's electricity, sometimes not. And there's no running water. No bathroom. No shower. Those are located somewhere in the gigantic shantytown, for the use of all the residents. In the summer, it's sweltering; in the winter, it's freezing. If this child is a bit luckier than most, his family might have some improvised means of heating in the winter. Often, it's a fire inside a can. The home fills with smoke, but at least it's not quite so cold. Sometimes a mishap occurs and a fire breaks out. The shacks are crowded together and there's no water nearby. A mishap like this frequently ends up burning down an entire neighborhood inside the ghetto.

Somehow this child grows up, though it's not clear how – at least judging by any criteria we're accustomed to. He lacks the nutrition, security, and stimuli children need. His menu is composed of one meal a day. At this meal, he eats a dark and sticky porridge that contains – maybe – some sort of legume and sometimes a bit of meat or something that was once a vegetable. There are no fresh vegetables. No fruit. Nonetheless, maybe this child is lucky, and he's not diseased and doesn't fall victim to sexual or physical violence in the streets, and he continues to grow. If he goes to school, it's a black-only school, which can't be compared to a school for white people. Perhaps his parents work, perhaps not. In any case, they must always carry a document detailing the limited area in which they are permitted to move around. And in these permitted areas, they are only allowed to use public transportation designated for black people, if such transportation even exists. If they're thirsty or hungry, they can only approach places for black people, if such places even exist. If they're tired, they have to search for a bench marked "Blacks Only" or "Nonwhites Only," although they'll probably only find benches marked "Whites Only" or "Europeans Only." Most jobs are off-limits to them, and they're compelled to make do with service jobs, working for white people. If they were lucky to receive some education, in an institution designated for black people only, of course, they must work only among the black population. Attempts to do something about their fate, through political organizing, for example, may exact a steep price, including violent retribution by the security forces, long periods of incarceration including forced labor, and sometimes death.

In Rwanda, in addition to the colonial exploitation and subjugation that stained the entire continent, there was also a unique variation on the "divide and conquer" policy – first by Germany (1898–1916) and then by Belgium (1916–62) – that fanned hatred between the two main ethnic groups in the country: the Hutu majority and the Tutsi minority. In 1994, after decades of political power struggles that were often accompanied by violence from both sides, which eventually escalated into civil war, the Hutus rose up against the Tutsis. The 100-day massacre was preceded by years of brainwashing in the media and months of meticulous preparation (after all, order is absolutely vital; in this case, 200,000 people were involved in the preparations) that included detailed lists with the names and addresses of those slated to be murdered. During the 100 days of the massacre, approximately – there's no exact number, only an estimate, so we can only use the nauseating estimate of "approximately" – a million men, women, and children were murdered. Most of them were Tutsis, though some were Hutus who were killed for defending the Tutsis or refusing to take part in the massacre. This means, if we break down the numbers to units of time the mind can comprehend, six people were murdered per minute, every minute, for 100 days. Planned and systematic rape, including deliberate infection with HIV, was also a weapon: approximately (again, a nauseating estimate) 500,000 women were raped; some of them were held as sex slaves during the months of the massacre. 20,000 children were born as a result of these rapes. When the bloodshed ended, two million people found themselves refugees, some of them Tutsis who fled the murderers, but many of them Hutus who fled acts of vengeance. And there were also over 100,000 orphans.

Here it is, again, in everyday terms: Unlike South Africa, which instituted separation between the white and nonwhite populations, no such separation ever existed in any community or framework in Rwanda. The human fabric of all the cities and villages, churches and markets, schools and places of work is composed of Hutus and Tutsis, an intertwined weave that is impossible to unravel. This means that enmity always simmered beneath the surface, even as the massacre lists were being prepared and "normal" life went on. This means that the crisis in trust that the victims experienced is deeper than we can imagine. This means that when the massacre was launched, a Tutsi man found himself, for example, being murdered – usually by a cold weapon such as a machete – by someone who had been his physician since birth; by his community priest, in whose choir he had sung as a child and whose sermons he had heard for as long as he could remember; by his neighbor; by someone who had been his friend until that day. This means that when the massacre was set in motion, a Tutsi woman found herself apprehended by her neighbors, with whom she had maintained good and even friendly neighborly relations until then, and delivered into the bloody hands of hate-crazed Hutu militiamen to satisfy their sexual urges and also, no less importantly, to infect her with HIV by men whose minds were so consumed with hatred that they were convinced of the need to spread the virus among as many Tutsi women as possible in order to annihilate everyone of that ethnic origin. This means that those in a position of influence in the community – for example the elders – were massacred first. This means that the rest were witnesses.

So much for the unique severity of "our" conflict, the one between Israelis and Palestinians. But let's stick with South Africa and Rwanda a bit longer, since, despite everything that happened, black and white South Africans reconciled, and Hutu and Tutsi Rwandans reconciled.

I want to make two more observations about the connection between the unique character of a conflict and the possibility of defusing it. The first pertains to the case in which Jewish-Israeli society can claim uniqueness: the Holocaust. Because here, too, reconciliation actually did take place: Israel and Germany maintain diplomatic relations, reparations agreements were signed, and a new and fresh generation of Israelis is renewing their grandparents' passports, traveling and even emigrating to Germany. The second observation demonstrates how – interestingly and perhaps contrary to what we tend to think – the full severity of an event can be portrayed without making any claim to exclusivity. The memorial museum in Rwanda presents the genocide that occurred there as a specific instance of a human phenomenon that repeated itself throughout the twentieth century. This does not at all diminish the significance and gravity of the Rwandan genocide; from a universal human perspective this may in fact intensify its horror, because the dynamics were known, the signs were there, and the warnings were sounded – yet, nonetheless, it occurred. It's interesting to note that among the other cases of genocide presented in the museum, the Holocaust is given the most central and extensive position.

It's difficult to deny that "our" conflict is challenging. While the stumbling block in South Africa and Rwanda was racial-ethnic, Israelis and Palestinians have also been awarded a territorial dispute and religious fervor. However, it seems to me that from the perspective of someone immersed in the maelstrom of the conflict, these factors are not tangibly linked to one's personal experience. After all, the pain of someone who has lost a person close to them is a personal, private pain, one that exists in the person's consciousness and, horribly, will continue to exist until they draw their last breath, even if the (religious, racial-ethnic, or territorial) conflict that caused it is resolved. Similarly, a person capable of looking at their enemy beyond the paradigm of "us" and "them" is able to do this because a shift has occurred in their personal, private consciousness. In this sense, those who've participated in a reconciliation process have more in common than they do not, because even if the context (place, time, reasons) is different, the profound psychological processes they underwent are similar. And this, in short, is what I tried to do in my meetings with people in South Africa and Rwanda: to learn what it means to reconcile and to distill the act of reconciliation down into its fundamental components; in other words, to discover what they came to understand – and what we still fail to comprehend.

But is that enough? Is it reasonable to assume, and permissible to hope, that if only we'd understand what they came to understand, we'd know what to do with this insight, despite the fact that history teaches that this is not always the case? This question, a natural, obvious byproduct of the attempt to understand, is constantly on my mind.

I raised this question with J, an astute, beautiful, gentle – but somewhat distant – woman who works as a senior researcher at the University of Rwanda. While she was typically thoughtful, patient, and open to collaborative thinking on any other subject we touched upon, my question concerning people's ability to learn something from the experience of others triggered a transformation in her. She became blunt, unequivocal, and emotional. "People don't learn from the mistakes of others," she told me sadly. "Look at history: human beings still fight wars against each other. And look at Rwanda: there were cases of genocide in the not-so-distant past and this still did not prevent it from happening here."

She spoke slowly and in a very soft voice, almost whispering, like someone who must put forth enormous physical effort to control the turmoil raging inside her. J is a Tutsi; perhaps the presence of my colleague H, a Hutu, intensified her inner turmoil and made the conversation, which was supposed to focus on a joint academic research topic, highly charged.

"But from their own mistakes," I pressed on, "people do learn?"

J turned her head toward H, and, in the most explicit display of ethnic tension I would encounter in Rwanda, asked, "What do *you* think, H, do people learn from their own mistakes?"

With a quiet and apologetic nod, without lifting his eyes from the floor, H signaled yes.

The question of whether human beings learn from others' mistakes remains an open one, as does the question regarding the human capacity for learning from the experience of those who've managed to reconcile. But what I do know is this: I won't give up trying. Because how many of us, while watching our adolescent children bang their heads against the wall just as we did at their age, can resist telling them about the mistakes we made, in the hope that perhaps this might spare them some suffering, even a little?

3

The Distance Between the Ideal and Reality

A REMARKABLE, HIGHLY MEANINGFUL SIMILARITY between South Africa and Rwanda: both societies praise their reconciliation process. A South African or Rwandan says "our reconciliation" with the same tone they might say "our children" or "our championship," a tone of proud ownership and identification. A similarity was also evident in the responses of South Africans and Rwandans to me, after I told them I'm Israeli. Despite the difference in each society's basic position toward Israel (critical in South Africa, sympathetic in Rwanda), the responses I got were tinged with condescension, however subtle. Sometimes it was implicit ("Hmmm," an extended silence, accompanied by an expressive look and an extended nod as well), and sometimes explicit ("Hmmm, you're the ones who still haven't managed to solve the *problems* between you, no?"). There's another similarity between the two societies, something more elusive and difficult to characterize, and this is a tone of relief of sorts that accompanies any conversation about what was and what almost was, were it not for choosing a different path. If I had to put it into words, it would sound like this: "We might not yet be where we want to be, but we're no longer *there*, inside the nightmare in which we were imprisoned." Reconciliation is a crucial component in the national identity of both societies despite the fact that neither country is without its difficulties, some of which stem from the conflict and its resolution. This is a point worth lingering on, because it's located at the core of the question: Is reconciliation actually possible?

In South African society there are outrageous, unimaginable gaps between eye-popping wealth (mostly among white people, sometimes among black citizens who have acquired wealth in recent years) and petrifying poverty (among black people); a high level of crime (mostly among black people who still live in ghettos); claims of unrestrained, sometimes corrupt, affirmative action by the new (black) government, also toward "colored" people, that is, the mixed-race and Asian populations, which partnered with the black majority in the struggle against apartheid and now find themselves excluded from positions of power.

Rwanda is not a democracy. This is not a result of the reconciliation process, so one cannot claim that this society paid for its reconciliation with democracy. Rwanda never was a democracy, and in fact such a thing has never really been on the agenda. But it's worth noting that reconciliation has been used by the government to justify actions that are inconsistent with human rights, even though there is no obvious conflict between human rights and reconciliation. The most basic level of individual freedom is absent: criticism of the regime will not be voiced in public spaces or on telephone calls. There is surveillance, and one pays a price for expressing critical positions. Coercive elements in the reconciliation process, which were initially viewed as necessary for bringing order to a bloody, fragmented society, remain in effect even though the formal process of reconciliation has ended. The crude distinction between victimizer (Hutu) and victim (Tutsi) has created warped situations. There are, for instance, Hutus who have become victims because they didn't take part in the slaughter, or because they suffered acts of revenge following the genocide. Yet they lack the legitimacy to speak out and are not recognized by the government or eligible for its support.

Despite this – and except for a frustrated, racist minority of white people in South Africa that still mourns its loss of power, and a Hutu minority that refuses to accept responsibility in the Rwandan case – reconciliation is considered a net good in both societies: the price for it was worth paying, the alternative was much worse. This view was expressed in every conversation I had with people, even with the more critical among them, even with those who feel that they personally paid an unfairly high price during the reconciliation process.

The distance separating the ideal of reconciliation and its reality is especially interesting in light of the difference between how reconciliation is understood in societies that went through such a process and how it is understood in a place like Israel. Neither South Africans nor Rwandans deny this distance, however much there's a readiness to acknowledge it in the former and a fear to do so in the latter. Regardless, in both societies the distance between ideal and reality has no bearing on their belief in this one essential fact: these are places where reconciliation has prevailed. The distance is not discouraging, nor does it nullify what has been achieved or its meaning and significance.

Why this shared perception in two very different societies? In my conversations with people in South Africa and Rwanda I encountered an insight – sometimes well-reasoned, sometimes intuitive – regarding the lofty nature of ideals: they are essentially unrealizable. In other words, the distance between the ideal and the reality of reconciliation is a given. All the same, this doesn't eliminate the possibility of reconciliation's fulfillment. This is in contrast to the prevailing view in Israel, according to which achieving anything less than ideal reconciliation serves as proof of its impossibility.

This insistence on purity, which serves as an excuse to do nothing, disturbs me, and not only because it shows us to be petty and sanctimonious. If you look away from the conflict, you'll discover that this Israeli desire for purity is selective. Do the tensions in Israeli society, which is internally divided, preclude the Talmudic principle "All of Israel are responsible for one another" or the possibility of Israelis loving their neighbor as themselves? Have we stopped striving for the solidarity that is derived from these ideals merely because our reality is not as rosy as they are? And what about gender equality? Does the fact that women continue to earn less than men and fill fewer senior positions, despite decades of equality before the law, discredit the ideal of equality or our aspiration for it?

There is still the question: *Is there a distance between ideal and reality that is too great?* Here's my answer: It's not about the size of the distance, but about a movement to close it, a movement that strives toward the ideal. After all, in the absence of movement even the smallest distance will remain. Whereas once there is movement, even a great distance can be covered.

Indeed, both South African and Rwandan societies continue to process and digest their reconciliation, sometimes openly and sometimes behind the scenes. This is difficult, ongoing work. A society that has gone through the reconciliation process is one that remains in a constant state of movement. From a linguistic perspective, it's more accurate to use the progressive tense of the verb when we think about South African and Rwandan societies: these are not societies that have reconciled; they are instead societies that are reconciling.

This reconciling state of mind, this continuous movement, stands in stark contrast to the apparent immobility I sometimes encountered in Africa, a contrast that accompanied me there and has stayed with me when I think about it in my office at home, here in Tel Aviv. Perhaps this contrast is a product of the difference between looking and listening. In the former, there is an active object and a passive subject, whereas in the second, both are active. It seems to me that this mutual, reciprocal action is what allows one to access another's narrative, which can open a tiny, precious crack in one's consciousness.

My time in Africa left me with a strong impression of walking, which was usually slow; of a constant presence, almost like the landscape itself, of people sitting or standing – in the street, at the entrance to a house or an office building, in a field, in the market – and looking around or contemplating something, but in either case for no apparent reason or purpose of the kind I'm used to; of long, fluid, uninterrupted movements of the body – motions that seemingly couldn't be broken up into their constituent parts. One of the foreigners I met in Rwanda, a reserved and idealistic young American man who ran an orphanage for street children, told me that it took him time to adopt this style that he called "motionless movement." As the sun beat down, he explained to me, in his dark suit that didn't seem to bother him at all, "If you move like that, it's not hot. Because of this, they're able to wear long pants and even sweaters when it's eighty-five degrees out, even more." I nodded with sweaty skepticism from inside my thin dress, and he offered me a haughty, distant, experienced smile. Even though he wasn't African, he was no longer really a *mzungu*, the name for a white person in the Bantu languages spoken in the region of the great lakes of Africa, a nickname whose literal meaning is "he who wanders aimlessly" or "he who wanders around himself and winds up in the same place."

Yet listening to the people I met in Africa had me picturing a path. I found that their stories – those tied to reconciliation as well as those about more day-to-day matters – often focused on the journey itself, as opposed to its outcome. This style of communication, in which the journey, and not the destination, is the point, might challenge one's patience. However, in light of our inverted Israeli reality, where the physical plane overflows with movement while the mind remains stuck, it might be worthwhile to linger a moment more on the meaning of movement in the context of reconciliation.

This sense of reconciliation involves, first and foremost, marking a goal and striving toward it. Such an orientation demands a patience that is often hard to summon, especially in the face of forces pulling us – at times successfully – backward, when each step away from the goal is seen as a failure, and as proof that the path is too long to be traveled.

Thoughts about reconciliation as movement take me back to Jali, the highest mountain in Kigali, and to a conversation there with a young man, B, that began when he approached me and asked – without introducing himself and without acknowledging the fact that I was in the middle of talking to six community health nurses about the nutrition of breastfeeding mothers – "Do you write all the time like that because you don't want to forget?" Our conversation continued like that, off and on, for the rest of the day. The green shades of the thick tropical vegetation on the mountain were rich and fleshy. The sky was open, the view breathtaking. Every afternoon during the rainy season there it storms, and the air grows dusty, the rain prickly. But when I arrived at the mountain in the early morning that day there was no sign of any of this yet, and it seemed the clear air and sights all around echoed with the eye-opening words spoken by B, who was captivated by what was happening – the building of a greenhouse and a pool of spirulina in the vegetable garden (what they call a "microgarden") at the mountain's community health center. This was a slightly larger vegetable garden than most of those attached to institutions and homes throughout the country, all of which are a central component of the government's efforts to fight the malnutrition afflicting approximately 40 percent of the Rwandan population. B was at my side throughout the day, with his ability to act as an interpreter – he spoke English and French in addition to Kinyarwanda, the local language – serving as an excuse. He simply ignored the fact that there was already an interpreter with me.

Even though the mountain is part of the city of Kigali, the area is distinctly rural. The roads are bumpy and rutted, and there are no sidewalks, traffic lights, or road signs. From time to time a car passes through, but one usually gets there on a dilapidated motorcycle-taxi, sometimes with a helmet, sometimes without. The car in which we arrived caused excitement among the schoolchildren we stopped near to ask for directions. Such an exchange can take some time, as a conversation of this sort, even when taking place between locals in their language, never sounds like: "Continue straight, turn left, and then right." Instead, there will be a few sentences from each side, thoughtful silence, shared uncertainty, and then a few more sentences, and sometimes the participation of additional people happening by, who will offer their own advice or ask questions. The complex melody of this exchange hints at the numerous, varied branches of the conversation. While the driver was busy discussing directions, the schoolchildren – some in shoes, some barefoot, but all of them in uniform – gathered around us. They momentarily abandoned their games with whatever was lying about, a soccer ball made from plastic bags stuffed into a net or a stick and a tire, and surrounded the car to reach an excited hand through the window toward us, thirsty for interaction. Our driver did not appear to leave the fact-finding mission regarding our destination with an unequivocal answer, but we nevertheless continued onward. Shakira's voice, tinny and fractured, perhaps coming from an untuned radio or battered stereo, burst forth from one of the many tiny houses, like a reminder of another world. The small houses, like the small vegetable gardens next to them, were clean and well cared for. Everything was extremely beautiful.

Rwandan poverty appears less derelict than in other places, a point worth dwelling on, as it represents unique features of Rwandan society that are also related to its reconciliation process. This is a society where inside and outside are almost two entirely separate and even dichotomous entities. That which appears well cared for from the outside is often meager or broken on the inside. Such is the case with the exterior of the houses versus their interiors, which often lack any infrastructure, or their vegetable gardens versus their malnutrition. This applies to the homes of the middle class and affluent as well. Appearance is also enormously important in the context of reconciliation. President Paul Kagame – who earned sympathy from the West during his first years in office, thanks to the reconstruction he led after the slaughter and the economic boom he created – leads this strategy with a firmness that is derived from his flexible, noncommittal approach to individual rights.

The closer one gets to the genocide, the narrower personal freedom becomes. Just mention it and the terms of the conversation close up with decisive uniformity. This voice of the chorus sounds something like: "It happened, we reconciled, there isn't one side and another side, we're all on the same side, partners in building a future." The ending is always the same, and it seems so obvious I found myself wondering again and again why it must be said at all. Perhaps it's because these words contain an additional, hidden layer: we're doing this for the next generation.

The uniformity of this voice, this chorus, made me uncomfortable, since it's the result of an undemocratic regime. The president was elected with over ninety percent of the vote, and the representatives of a single political party dominate all aspects of the individual's life. Growing a well-tended micro-garden is not optional, much as reconciliation isn't, and never was, a matter of choice.

I HAVE AN URGE to make a grating sound whenever the chorus sings. I usually restrain myself, because I can identify the emotional role this collective voice plays, the reason it was formed, what it defends – but the urge is there and has been there as long as I can remember.

I spent most of my school years in Canada and the United States, which suggests that my urge to be this grating voice has nothing to do with Israeli society in general or the Israeli-Palestinian conflict in particular. I sensed, even if it wasn't in a manner I could express in words, that a person's feelings should flow from within and not be dictated by a common emotion arrived at through some deductive, coercive process.

As a seven-year-old girl in Canada, the custom of starting the morning by singing the national anthem puzzled me, and the flag hanging from its pole in the corner of the classroom only intensified this feeling of estrangement. Something that *everyone* is doing in the *same way* at the *same time* can't be OK, I thought. Suspicious at the very least. I didn't want to offend anyone, so I didn't cause a fuss. I stood each morning with the rest of the children, but I didn't really sing the anthem. I lowered my head and looked at the floor or my shoes as if there was something truly interesting there. No one noticed (or maybe someone did notice but thought it wasn't important enough to bother with, and if there was in fact someone like that, I wish I could go back to that time and place to thank them).

As a slightly older but still young girl, now a ten-year-old in New York, I went to an Orthodox religious school, where praying was the most important thing. In truth, the place was largely preoccupied with appearances. Again and again, I was surprised by the extent to which everyone participated in the pretense of religious piety for social reasons, even though it did not align with the outlook of most of the students and their families. Until then, I hadn't concerned myself with questions about God. As I said, I was ten, and the subject simply hadn't come up before, but this unified voice caused me real and constant bodily discomfort. In fact, the atmosphere of coercion surrounding prayer at this school caused my vague sensations to sprout into a less intuitive and more informed inquiry into questions of faith. The disgust – and it really was disgust – that my questions gave rise to among some of the school faculty became the fertilizer, water, and light for these sprouts. I again found myself preoccupied with the question of how it could be that *everyone* feels and thinks the *same thing* at the *same time*, and that this time is determined by some directive, whereas what one feels or thinks can only be a *personal* thing that emerges from within. This seemed very odd to me, even illogical, but this time, too, loyal (or bound) to my desire not to offend anyone,

I did nothing offensive. I employed that same unsophisticated tactic of lowering my gaze and moving my lips in imitation of singing without joining in the prayer. (These movements, usually, echoed my inner speech – internal dialogues I conducted with other people, though my actual conversations with them in real life were much less interesting or satisfying.) But absent here was that adult whom I like to imagine saw all this and decided years earlier to let me skip the singing of the anthem, so one day I was called to the office of the principal, a dour rabbi who spoke to me in a pious, supposedly tolerant tone, that of someone who is certain that his progressiveness is proven by his decision to invite me to this talk prior to punishing me. "I notice that you are not *really* praying with everyone," he said. "I see that you're only acting *as if* you are with your lips." My forehead burned and my mouth went dry. I understood I was in trouble. "It's true," I answered. The option of lying absolutely never occurred to me. "I don't really pray but that's because I don't feel a *need* to pray." The rabbi's nostrils widened. Apparently, I felt a need to explain myself, and despite the fear, which was being channeled into a truly violent thirst, I added that I didn't understand why it was important for me to pray, because "even if God exists, why would he care about what I do, I'm really not that important." Even these words, which in retrospect I can see were experienced as a needle through his heart, were spoken innocently, as I had hope that perhaps they would lead to a conversation on the matter. But in that moment, in the precise moment I spoke the words "even if God exists," I had cast doubt on a thing not to be doubted, and the conversation with the rabbi was over. He passed his objections about my behavior on to my parents and never again spoke a word to me, not even when he passed me in the halls, though he made it a habit to position himself right across from me during prayers to stare at my lips in order to confirm whether their movements corresponded to the words of the prayer.

For me the voice of the chorus is a sign of discord, because if it weren't for discord there would be no need for such unison.

This discord is what I listen for. I listen for the people who, were they a floor, would be a creaky one. It's hard to find them, but in Rwanda there are those who don't obey the voice of the chorus. They're interesting, especially in the context of our stubborn conflict, because they show that our simplistic view of reconciliation (the ideal or nothing at all) is getting in the way. In Rwanda it's understood that there's an artificial, forced element to their reconciliation. In fact, it derives from a concept that I think most of us can relate to: there are things that cannot be forgiven, there are things a person will never get over. The reconciliation of the generation that experienced the genocide is not an objective, it's a means. It is unbearable, and at times even intensifies the trauma of that generation – and, based on what we know from the difficulties experienced by the second generation of the Holocaust, that of their own children – but it's done so that the next generations are born into a different reality.

One of those other voices, echoing in the gap between the ideal and the reality of reconciliation, emerged in the voice of B, a tall, handsome man in whose eyes was a combination of voracious childish curiosity and a deep, somehow distant skepticism, of the sort you find in an old person who has experienced a thing or two in life. He wore green coveralls and a pair of Chuck Taylors; his body language spoke with a confident, playful self-awareness. My conversation with B took place on two levels. On one he recited the voice of the chorus; on the other he checked my responses, while slowly, carefully, and quietly, a subversive tone entered his speech.

"What are those letters?" he gestured with his chin toward my hand, writing in my notebook.

"Hebrew."

"?" he signaled wordlessly.

"The language of Jesus and the Old Testament."

"Really, backwards like that? Interesting. What do you think about Jesus?" he probed, his glance adding untold layers to his question.

"A fascinating figure," I answered, "literarily, morally, historically. But I'm an atheist," I added quietly, so as not to embarrass him in case others could hear, aiming to respond to what wasn't asked but which I sensed was passing from him to me, like bass notes one doesn't hear so much as feel as a tremor in the floor.

My answer sent his frantic gaze searching all around us. After he confirmed that we were speaking in private, he said: "Really? You mean you don't believe in God?"

"Yes."

He nodded for a while. "Me neither," he said very softly. "I mean, I go to church, like everyone in Rwanda. My parents, one's Catholic and one's Pentecostal, they're very religious. I go and I pray but I don't believe in God because I ask myself where he was during the genocide. What, he was *taking a break* just then? Same thing with your genocide, of the Jews, no?"

B was silent for a moment, but before I could answer, he said: "We're short on wood. For the greenhouse," he motioned with his head in the direction of a nearby grove. "Let's go get some."

We weren't actually short on wood. But we were nearing the topic that demanded caution, so he searched for a safe space to talk. We walked – B and I and a boy no older than twelve who worked there like one of the adults – over to the adjacent eucalyptus grove. The boy, it quickly became clear, only understood Kinyarwanda, and B felt safe speaking to me with him around. B pointed to this or that branch, and the boy chopped it off with a few blows from a machete, the same tool used as a murder weapon during the days of the massacre, which (in a manner that never ceased to astound me) remains in regular use all over, everyone ignoring the metamorphosis it underwent during the massacre.

B pointed for the boy and spoke to me, pointed and spoke. The boy struck the trees and from time to time lifted his gaze toward the strange goings-on he couldn't understand. I walked behind them and listened to B's words, which flowed like a liquid that had found a crack in an otherwise sealed container.

When the massacre broke out, B's parents were in the Congo. He was five and, together with his younger brother, remained with his grandmother, his aunt, and her two small sons. Mount Jali, as mentioned before, is the highest mountain in Kigali, and for strategic reasons it was important for the Hutu militia fighters to control it.

"It was great luck," he explained without a trace of irony, "because they were busy with their patrolling, drinking, and raping, so they didn't have much time to look for us." He and his relatives hid for three days behind rocks and bushes. "I couldn't help it and was looking about all the time," he said, and I could picture the boy he was, with the same curious and hungry gaze he has today. "There were hacked off limbs scattered everywhere," he continued, "a lot of decapitated heads too. Sometimes their eyes were wide open. And many puddles of blood. After a while the earth absorbed the blood, leaving dark stains behind."

After three days they were discovered. B and his relatives tried to escape from the militia fighters who fell upon them armed with machetes, but his grandmother was old, the children were children, and the aunt – she adjusted her pace to that of her mother, children, and nephews. When the fighters started closing in on them and it was clear they had no chance, his grandmother instructed her family: "Run." And she turned and faced their pursuers. "She ran straight to them," B said, "like a girl running into a parent's open arms," he said with his arms spread like a father ready to receive his child and wrap her in a hug. So, as they cut her limbs from her body with machetes and her screams died out, he, his brother, his aunt, and his cousins fled.

B continued talking, as if in a trance. "The Hutu militia fighters decided to cleanse the mountain of any Tutsi presence, and whoever wasn't slaughtered in the early days was expelled in long marches. We had to walk one behind the other. Whoever stepped out of line, even just to hold someone's hand, they removed him from the procession and murdered him on the spot, in front of everyone. My little brother was afraid and he wanted to hold my hand, so I held his hand behind my back and forced him to stay right there. The whole time he wanted to be next to me, and I kept him behind me. Every once in a while they took someone out of the line, even if he hadn't left it, just because, because one of the militiamen felt like killing or raping someone. I was curious and watched all the time. The things I saw, you can't imagine . . . such things." He shook his head from side to side. "It's unimaginable."

He doesn't know how many days it took to walk to the refugee camp, where their parents found them. "They didn't believe they'd find us alive." He recalled with excitement the moment of seeing them again. "They cried and clapped, cried and clapped," he said and showed me. "They had thought we too were murdered on the mountain."

They spent long months in the refugee camp. When they returned to the mountain everything had been destroyed, and they continued living as displaced people here, in the community medical center where we were working hard that day to build a greenhouse.

We – B, the boy, and I – went back to the greenhouse that was gradually being built, and placed the unnecessary eucalyptus beams there.

In the years after that massacre, he continued, he would go to the gacaca hearings – the community courts established as part of the reconciliation apparatus – and watch those who confessed their crimes and asked for forgiveness and those who listened and gave it. He spoke freely now, out loud, apparently because his words now matched those of the chorus.

"Gacaca comes from the word *umucaca*," he explained, "which is grass so soft that people come to sit on it, because this way of solving problems has always existed in Rwanda: you sit on the grass and you listen to each other and the community members help you to reach a solution. Those who stayed in jail are the stubborn ones who don't want to ask for forgiveness," he added, and knocked a fist against his head.

"And does it work?" I muttered. "That is, people asked for forgiveness and people forgave them and everyone succeeded in putting the past behind them? I mean . . ." I squirmed, "the reconciliation is real? The Hutu and Tutsi lived, and still live, in mixed communities. Which means that the slaughterers and the slaughtered and their children meet in the market, at the store, in church, and at work. Every day. All the time."

He thought a moment, like someone trying to find a way to get through to me and my thick head, and then he motioned with his chin to the young man who sat on a stone not far from us, staring at the darkening horizon. This man was not within hearing distance from us. Still, B returned to a whisper, just to be safe, as here again his voice left that of the chorus. In Rwanda it's forbidden to speak about someone's ethnic affiliation.

"He and I, the two of us are Tutsi," he whispered, "we have a cooperative, we grow mushrooms. And our partner," he motioned with his eyes to another man who took part in building the greenhouse, young as well, "he's Hutu. And not just any Hutu," B said. "His father murdered my grandmother. He confessed to what he did at the gacaca, but I knew about this even before then because I saw him, I saw him cut my grandmother to pieces."

I tried again, because it was truly incomprehensible. "OK, I understand you're partners, but what I'm asking is, are you friends?"

"Sure," he answered.

I wouldn't let this go, even though I knew I was being difficult, or at least I thought I was: "And you trust him?"

"Completely," he answered in the assured voice of the chorus, almost as if he were reciting something. "It happened. We reconciled. There isn't one side and another. We are all on the same side, partners in building the future." But after a moment he again whispered: "Of course, of course for our parents it's hard. For them it's nearly impossible. But they do it for us. You understand?"

I heard similar tones in the voice of a woman in her sixties, also Tutsi, whose family was entirely wiped out in the genocide, and in the voice of a man her age, for whom the usual difficulty of talking about the subject was compounded by the discomfort of being a member of the Hutu tribe. He probably felt a question mark hovering over him at all times regarding what he did, or didn't do, at that time. With their words they illuminated those regions of the mind where reconciliation is almost an oxymoron. On the face of it, these are the unspoken regions in the reconciling society of Rwanda, but it seems to me that they're actually quite present in the saying "It's for the next generation" – so commonly voiced by the chorus. This saying, seemingly unnecessary since it states the obvious, is said like a calming, consoling mantra, because it signals something that those who reconcile need, at times desperately, to be acknowledged: there are situations in which reconciliation is unbearably difficult. This saying positions the next generation as the reason for everything. It puts the reconciliation process on a timeline and thus enables its existence, even when the work is not yet complete. The next generation makes logical that which on the face of it appears to defy logic altogether.

4

Between Romanticism and Pragmatism

IN SOUTH AFRICA, the authority that established reconciliation as a goal was embodied in a leader of moral stature. Reconciliation was part of his humanistic worldview. In Rwanda, by contrast, reconciliation was the means by which a dictator, one who had a hand in past atrocities, could rebuild a devastated country. Perhaps fittingly, the reconciliation processes that these two societies went through were as different from each other as day and night. And probably no less different than the one we will go through, if we ever choose to. However, it is precisely because these two processes sit at opposite ends of the reconciliation spectrum that it's interesting to consider those ingredients they do share. These common denominators may be a kind of necessary minimum for the existence of reconciliation, and thus perhaps a point of departure for us.

Man: Shaped by the Winds of Time

At the southern tip of Africa, the Indian and Atlantic Oceans meet. Viewed from the summit of Table Mountain in Cape Town, their meeting is dramatic. The wind in Cape Town is also dramatic, appearing suddenly, sometimes with such strength that it drowns out all other sounds. In some places there are pockets where the wind blows with incredible force. The trees that grow there lean in the direction of the wind, their trunks rising only slightly above the ground and then growing sideways, almost parallel to it. I have long wondered: How similar are we humans and these windswept trees that are shaped and even stunted in their growth by the winds of time? Quite a bit, it turns out.

Once you dive into the reconciliation processes of South Africa and Rwanda, you see that there was little romanticism involved. There's also not much to be romantic about in the reality that has followed. But before I touch on all that, I'd like to pause for a moment on the individual, including the one who reconciles. After all, if reconciliation is first and foremost a matter of goal setting, then it is an action that someone has to take. Is this someone an individual led by some understanding or insight? Is it one individual and then another and then another, all joining together in a critical mass that eventually acquires unstoppable historical momentum?

If the answer stems from my idea of humanity – then yes. But if it comes from the reality of reconciling societies – then not exactly. The reconciliation processes of Rwanda and South Africa differ from each other in many ways, but there is one difference that I wish to dwell on. This difference touches on one of the crucial existential questions, certainly in modern times, and that is the degree of one's freedom. The Rwandan reconciliation process – which was imposed from above and carried out as if it were law – involved little freedom, while the South African one – which was the result of a democratic decision and a shared process – involved much more. However, despite what we might like to think – despite what I would like to think, if we step back for a moment to the notion of the distance from the ideal – we see that the two processes exist on the same continuum. Except among those few who were able to find the motivation within themselves, in both instances an external force was required to lead and convince, to educate and sometimes even to coerce. In both cases, the engine was a superego embodied by a political, moral, or religious authority that conceptualized reconciliation in the context of the particular conflict in question. The picture that emerges from observing these reconciliation processes (and others) is that of individuals who perform the action, that is, choose reconciliation, but who do so mostly out of obedience to an authority external to them. This authority takes various forms, but its main purpose is to create a space in which individuals can take the leap of faith, something I'll discuss later.

What does this say about human nature? Well, it says things we already know, both intuitively and historically: humans tend to seek out authority, and, moreover, we (also) have impulses that contradict sublime values.

It's unpleasant to consider the human hunger for authority, since human history is full of examples where external forces led societies not to reconciliation but to catastrophe. Nevertheless, as history teaches, this characteristic is a given. It also seems to me true that even those parts of human nature that resist authority do so in response to it, that is, in response to an entity external to them. This entity therefore always exists, and is embodied in authority – political, religious, or moral – which, to return to the subject at hand, can conceptualize reconciliation but can also conceptualize strife or the impossibility of reconciliation (these latter two possibilities are in fact different versions of the same thing).

It is also unsettling to think about those impulses and patterns in human nature that are not sublime and in some cases even contradict the sublime. This challenges what we are accustomed to thinking of as human nature. However, if we consider a more complete picture of the human being and, more precisely, those human characteristics that most of us find appealing, it seems that they are (also) the result of a civilizing process. Though this process may or may not have eradicated those negative impulses (one could argue both sides here), humans have for the most part learned to restrain them. Most of us don't take things from each other just because we feel like it, we don't have sex with our family members, and we don't kill everyone we don't like. Even in the more subtle realms of interpersonal relations, we can see that most of us don't pick our noses when we dine with others, and that we generally give up our seat on public transportation to someone older than us. We like to think that this is simply the way we are, but such behavior is also a consequence of the same process through which humans came to agree among themselves about what lies outside the realm of the socially acceptable. In the tension between policing and persuasion, between coercion and influence, between brainwashing and education, these agreements have been internalized to the point that they are mostly perceived as natural limitations accepted by all. We no longer remember that humans decided to accept and practice such restraints until they became second nature.

A similar process occurs in reconciling societies: those human impulses opposed to reconciliation become defined as those that should remain outside the realm of the socially acceptable. Then, in an ongoing process, the members of this society practice this restraint until it seems a necessary and natural product of common sense.

A person's obedience – and more precisely, their degree of freedom – has another aspect, one expressed in the relationship between the collective and the individual. Put differently, how far does an individual's obedience to the collective's narrative reach, and to what extent can the collective reasonably demand this obedience from the individual? The full gravity of this question is felt in reconciling societies, perhaps because there is an expectation of some overlap between the values that underlie and motivate reconciliation and those that prioritize the individual and their well-being. And perhaps here we note some of the difficulty that such a process poses for us: it contradicts our self-image as individualistic beings, as well as the belief that our society grants us a relatively high degree of freedom. However, this self-image is based on parts of ourselves that we deny (more on that in a moment). It is also a self-image that makes it difficult for us to derive anything of value from reconciliation processes in societies that we perceive as less individualistic than our own. We are, simply put, skeptical of the relevance for us of *that kind* of process in *that kind* of society.

As for the questions of how exactly social agreements are reached, and their essence as representatives of one set of values or another, I will just say this: what matters here is the tension between the collective and the individual, or more precisely, the extent to which the collective is allowed to demand that the individual suspend his or her emotions in favor of the collective narrative. This is a question that produces meaningful answers only when it challenges the individual, that is, when an agreement emerges that is consistent with the individual's values. In this context, my encounters with reconciliation in South Africa and Rwanda was challenging, as it left me with the feeling that despite everything (or in other words: despite the distance from the ideal in both places), the reconciliation achieved there (or, perhaps more accurately, the reconciliation that is being achieved there) brought both societies to a situation that was infinitely better than the one they were in before. In South Africa, nonwhite citizens gained democracy, equality before the law, and a moral victory, as well as a victory for their narrative, while white citizens' moral standing was repaired, allowing them to return to the family of nations. In Rwanda, both sides gained equality before the law and the practical possibility of living in their country or returning to continue their lives there. Without further warfare, everyone secured a space where there is hope for a better future and where, in the most substantive way, people have real possibilities.

In terms that are harder to quantify, those of the soul and the spirit, everyone has secured a space where dreaming is possible, a space where that part of the person that is unique and singular – and not, or not only, characterized by their relationship to their group in the conflict – can be revealed or rediscovered. Precisely because of this, I found myself confronting the personal price exacted from individuals in these societies. This price is not easy to digest, not only because of the demand for conformity but because it contradicts something in our logic – the impossibility of doing justice (or, depending on the observer's position, giving up the demand for justice) in the most concrete sense. This price precludes correcting injustices rooted in the apartheid regime in South Africa, for example. This price silences the voices of Rwandan victims whose trauma still screams within them but who are asked to stifle this scream by their society's demand and perhaps also by their own imperative that has internalized the spirit of this new era.

If we return to the self-image of Israelis, we'll see that this society can operate like a well-oiled machine, too, inside of which individuals obediently fulfill their roles. In the 1990s, the state of Israel was alarmed that the Sea of Galilee was drying up. Saving water became a national project. "National project" is a term that isn't exactly music to my ears, regardless of my position on that particular project, whose effectiveness in this case was both impressive and disturbing. The educational system operated as any education system can when it defines a clear goal for itself in a few simple words. In those years I couldn't brush my teeth without one of my daughters suddenly appearing and turning off the tap. In TV commercials, children appeared suddenly and turned off the tap on their parents who were brushing their teeth. The media was mobilized to meticulously monitor the level of the Sea of Galilee and to share horror stories about the possible consequences were it to dry up. Even the private sector contributed, by offering water meters for taps and toilets. There was little doubt in the public discourse of those years. Most of us welcomed the project into our private spaces and complied, even if some of us allowed ourselves to cut corners with an occasional full flush of the toilet without any real justification.

In this instance, the atmosphere of conformity only led to minor restrictions on the individual and a little discomfort (just a little, and only among certain parts of society, probably not many). However, in the name of the collective we have also made sacrifices much greater and more substantive than turning off the tap while brushing our teeth. Silencing ourselves, for example. Here, too, we don't have to go too far back in time to realize that the distance between what our society was willing to demand from some of us and what Rwandan society is willing to demand from some of their citizens is smaller than we think, and perhaps smaller than we would like to remember. In Israeli society during the early years of the state, there was no place for the horrors of the Holocaust. To be more precise, there was a place for the Holocaust, but only as a historical *event*, not as a personal experience that a survivor could introduce into this new *Israeliness*, which was self-perceived as healthy and strong. Survivors' expressions of trauma were perceived as the opposite of the new Israeli. Such expressions were sometimes seen as madness, so survivors' personal stories were censured at both the societal level and the individual level. As the years have passed, and not so many have, this has come to seem absurd, painful, outrageous even. Yet it's not hard to understand that the new Israeli society could not face these elements within it without undermining its own stability. Might we conclude from this that when this traumatic content finally emerged, the system – the Israeli collective – was strong enough to contain it? And if this is accurate, might it be reasonable to claim that the temporary denial of the trauma allowed the new society to be built? And, following this same line of thought, can we then view, for example, those suppressed parts of the Rwandan genocide trauma in the same nearly therapeutic way?

It seems to me that it's *possible* to view the question of forced repression in the context of the "generation of the desert," which I mentioned earlier in the case of the generation of the Holocaust and the founding of the modern state of Israel. It is the generation that is forced to repress its trauma based on the assumption (informed or intuitive) that when the repressed contents resurface – and at some point they always do – the next generation will be the one to deal with it. And this generation will be – maybe, hopefully – a little less damaged and better able to bear it. It is *possible* to look at the question of silencing this way, but it is not necessary and perhaps not even relevant to do so, since psychological analysis and a study of the results are not enough to justify it morally. The question remains: To what extent are societal demands on the individual within it morally justifiable? It seems to me that one's answer will always be influenced by one's attitude toward the collective and its narrative. I only wish to draw attention to the fact that at times here in Israel, too, in the tension between the individual and the collective, the latter comes out on top. In other words: this social mechanism exists, the only question is what it is applied to. Therefore, the argument that the prices paid in South Africa and Rwanda are irrelevant to our own society does not stand up to scrutiny.

However, I would like to argue that despite the not very romantic image of the person being shaped by the wind of the times like those stunted trees in Cape Town, individual choice still exists. The recognition of a need does not dictate the specific manner in which this need will be filled; this is something that – hopefully, and to the extent that society permits – each person chooses. Recognizing something as a need makes a person more aware and therefore actually strengthens their ability to choose. If we look for a moment at one of the basic needs of human existence – the need for communication and human touch, for example – we find that recognizing this need generally allows us to choose more intelligently and accurately who the people close to us will be; that is, how this need will be fulfilled. Society, circumstances, and character determine human beings' degree of freedom, but to one degree or another, we are creatures of choice. And at any given moment we choose which of our needs – some sublime, some less so – to obey and in what manner. Therefore, the question is not *whether* we will obey, but rather in *what way* we fulfill the need to obey. Each person has the option of choosing what (that is, which ideals) and who (that is, which entity that embodies them) to obey.

The process of civilization is ongoing. Humans strive to improve themselves as individuals and as members of society, and strive to improve the society in which they live. Reconciliation, with all the limitations it demands, is part of that process, and this is where the element of choice comes into play: just as at any given moment we choose which of our needs to obey and in what way to obey them, so we choose which internal or external command to obey, and we can choose the one that embodies the possibility of reconciliation. For the choice to be informed, or, more precisely, conscious, it is essential that we know how to identify – within ourselves, within our environment, and certainly within those parts of our environment that claim to be our source of authority – what and who can bring us closer to our goal. We'll come back to this later.

South Africa: Black and White, and Difficult Nonetheless

On the surface, there were two separate processes that changed the face of South Africa. First, negotiations between the white government and the organizations fighting for equality, led by the African National Congress (ANC), which resulted in free elections and thus the end of the rule of the white minority over the black and colored majority. Second, national reconciliation within the framework of the Truth and Reconciliation Commission established by the new South African government and based on the negotiated agreements.

Indeed, the apartheid regime came to an end because international pressure, together with rising violence and a dead-end state of mind on the domestic front, forced the government – in an uneven and fitful process marked by painful disillusionment – to recognize that something had to change. And this regime came to an end thanks to the sense of responsibility of the leaders – Frederik Willem de Klerk on the white side and Nelson Mandela on the black – who signaled the end of apartheid as their goal. Despite wrathful prophecies about black people rising up against their former oppressors in a bloodbath, these men led the country to what was almost unimaginable – an orderly transfer of power from white to black hands.

But the end of apartheid and reconciliation are intertwined, in two senses. First, reconciliation could not have taken place if apartheid had not ended. Second, Mandela, who led the struggle to end apartheid and became the country's leader after it, saw both as deeply meaningful and intertwined components of the same concept of justice. He didn't stop when he won what he fought for: equality. He continued to strive toward what was for him the ultimate goal: reconciliation.

The struggle of black and colored people for equal rights began with the establishment of the apartheid regime, when the right-wing National Party came to power in 1948 and began to enshrine in legislation its view of the superiority of white people over all other people. The laws of segregation and discrimination were gradually deepened and expanded: the prohibition against "mixed" marriages and interracial sexual relations, registration by race in the census, demarcation of residential areas by race and the prohibition against nonwhite people from living in cities, restriction of movement, segregation on the basis of race in the use of public facilities and the prohibition against entry to most of them for nonwhite people, the establishment of a low level of education for nonwhite people, the prohibition against filling senior positions by nonwhite people, and the denial of full citizenship to nonwhite people. The struggle for equality, led by the ANC, was initially nonviolent, and was carried out in the political arena and in the media as well. However, starting in the 1960s, and mainly as a result of events in Sharpeville, where sixty-nine black demonstrators were shot dead at a nonviolent rally, along with Prime Minister Hendrik Verwoerd's decision to ignore a letter from Mandela – in which the latter urged the former to convene a national conference at which all

South Africans would be represented in order to draft a new, democratic and non-racial constitution – the struggle grew more militant and came to include acts of sabotage and terrorism.

The white apartheid regime responded by outlawing these organizations, including the ANC, and persecuting their leaders and activists, including Mandela. Security forces were mobilized to fight the resistance organizations, as were government and law enforcement officials, who in many cases committed gross human rights violations. Activists were held in administrative detention for long periods without trial, and suspects were violently interrogated and tortured, sometimes to the point of death. Many such deaths went unreported, as cover-ups and evidence tampering were widespread. White citizens who supported the anti-apartheid struggle were called traitors and were persecuted as well, while the government did everything in its power to prevent dialogue between white intellectuals and businessmen and ANC representatives. The government defended this policy with the legal pretext that one should not enter into talks with an illegal organization, and with the security pretext that any dialogue with ANC members would endanger the country's security. When the opposition attempted to circumvent these restrictions by meeting in neighboring countries, the apartheid regime responded with bureaucratic interference such as withholding passports.

Tensions in the country increased. Demonstrations by black and colored people were brutally suppressed, resulting in the deaths of many protesters. The government responded by declaring a state of emergency throughout the country. Such blatant human rights violations drew the attention of the international community. Developing countries preceded Western countries in criticizing the apartheid regime and subsequently in imposing sanctions against it. An international arms embargo was imposed on the country and gradually expanded. By 1987 South Africa had become the target of worldwide economic and cultural sanctions. Shamefully, Israel was the only democratic country that did not agree to participate in the sanctions and joined only following massive pressure from the United States, pressure that included a threat to cut off American aid. In the 1950s and '60s, Israel had actually taken a clear stand against apartheid, but this stance had changed in 1973, when many African countries severed their ties with Israel in the wake of the Yom Kippur War. In response, Israel had sought out new allies on the continent.

The sanctions took their toll, and in the final period of the apartheid regime, its leaders, led by President P. W. Botha, behaved as if they had a hidden understanding – deep in their consciousness and under thick layers of denial – that they could not continue like this. As is the custom of those whose inner self is conflicted, this government assumed a pragmatic position. According to this approach, concessions were the "price" that had to be paid in order to preserve the ideological veneer keeping power in their hands. Such concessions were not made due to any ethical position, one that might have seen apartheid as a moral injustice that needed to be eliminated. Thus, the government waged a war of attrition that was an expression of its false consciousness. While one hand "threw bones" to black and colored people in an attempt to appease them and the international community, the other continued to justify apartheid's continued existence by asserting the impossibility of talking to the ANC.

Thus, during the 1980s, some "petty apartheid" regulations were abolished: the prohibition against nonwhite people using public parks, benches, toilets, public telephone booths designated for white people only, etc. Nevertheless, the foundations of apartheid, in particular the prohibition against voting and seeking election, remained in place. Attempts to start negotiations between the government and the ANC were undertaken both at home and abroad. Outside South Africa, countries and international organizations tried to play the role of mediator. Domestic efforts involved a stunningly complex secret channel that found the imprisoned Mandela at one end and Hendrik Coetsee – the minister of justice, who was also in charge of the police and prisons – at the other, with five "degrees of separation" between them. The formulas offered to the parties were in fact what would be agreed to a few years later, but conservative white leaders within the government and the ruling party opposed it. President Botha, nicknamed "The Old Crocodile" due to his obsession with maintaining his image as someone immune to pressure, was imprisoned by his fear of showing weakness. And so, time and again, attempts at dialogue remained in the realm of "almost."

To justify these failures, the security forces intensified their operations against the ANC, including attacks on their bases in neighboring countries. Meanwhile, the government focused on delegitimizing the ANC and Mandela by asserting that they were violent by nature. According to this seemingly simple logic, it was thus impossible to talk to the ANC, let alone grant equality to nonwhite people. President Botha demonstrated this impenetrable circular logic upon his return from Europe, where he met with a Bavarian minister, one of South Africa's last remaining friends. Acting like someone who had made a discovery whose greatness was indisputable, Botha proudly shared the solution he had devised: he would offer Mandela release from prison if he declared that violence was not a legitimate tool for achieving political goals. In other words, Mandela would overturn the ANC's 1961 decision to pursue armed struggle. If he did not agree – and it was clear he would not, since Mandela was not being offered anything substantive in return, not even the legalization of the ANC itself – the "true face" of the organization and its leader would be exposed. The entire world would once again realize that there was no one to talk to. Botha also attempted to trap Mandela by making dialogue conditional on two additional demands. The first of these was to renounce the Communist Party, which had been an ally of the ANC throughout the years of its struggle. The second demanded that Mandela declare a willingness to give up the principle of majority rule. Instead, he would settle for a power-sharing arrangement based on equality between ethnic groups, thereby ignoring the actual demographics of the country.

But these attempts did not achieve their desired result, not in the eyes of the international community nor in those of the people fighting for equality at home. This outcome wouldn't have surprised any outside observer, but the leaders of the government were astonished by it. Simply put, offering limited (if not altogether insignificant) changes to the apartheid regime or highlighting the violent nature of the black and colored struggle for equality couldn't eliminate the crux of the matter: discrimination between people on the basis of race. The government's efforts to get the international community to recognize the difficulties they faced in dealing with the terrorism of freedom fighters were also unsuccessful. International sanctions were tightened, South Africa found itself isolated, and domestic violence only increased. Similar to what happened in the Soviet Union following perestroika, Botha's willingness to truncate apartheid in a desperate attempt to preserve it had the opposite effect: the "bones" he threw fueled the hopes of black and colored people that ending apartheid was possible. In the final years of the apartheid regime, its leaders and supporters lost confidence. They felt misunderstood, their frustration grew, and they behaved with a hysteria somewhat reminiscent of an abusive husband who realizes that his wife is slipping away from him.

In 1989, Botha resigned under pressure from his party following a stroke. Disappointed that his pragmatic stance was not accepted by black and colored South Africans and the world, he made way for de Klerk, also a member of the National Party, who was elected precisely because he was conservative. Nothing in his personality or worldview hinted at what was to come.

In his first speech to parliament as president, de Klerk surprised the world and South Africa – already fed up with the regime's promises of reform – by announcing that he now recognized that the apartheid policy had failed. It is difficult to overstate the importance of his words, in particular his use of the verb "recognize." De Klerk expressed nothing less than a profound change in consciousness: no more changes to the existing system, but a recognition that this system no longer had a right to exist. All the same, his choice to use "failure" is also significant, as it presents apartheid not as a moral error but as a political failure. This distinction has far-reaching implications when it comes to the matter of forgiveness. More on that later.

De Klerk's announcement came as an earthquake. If in the United States, equality for black people meant their full participation in the systems of government, it was thus clear in South Africa that the end of apartheid meant the transfer of power to the black majority. This portrait of reality played on the deepest fears of the white minority, even its moderates, who imagined the black majority taking power and launching a campaign of revenge against the white minority. De Klerk didn't limit himself to words. In the same speech he announced the restoration of the legal status of the outlawed parties (first and foremost the ANC), the abolition of the death penalty, the release of hundreds of political prisoners, the limiting of administrative detentions to six months, and his willingness to enter into negotiations with all parties in order to draft a new constitution in which all sides would enjoy equality. A week later, he announced the release of Nelson Mandela from prison after twenty-seven years.

This dramatic statement was the result of de Klerk's understanding that only a quantum leap could free South Africa from the paralysis that gripped it and throw his opponents – both within his party and among the resistance organizations – off balance. Indeed, alongside the excitement and hopes that swept the country, conservative white people felt betrayed. Their own flesh and blood had chosen a path that, in their eyes, was nothing less than ethnic suicide. Three hundred and fifty years of living on the continent had severed them from their European roots, and they saw themselves as sons and daughters of the continent, a native ethnic group that had a natural, divine right to the land, a group that now had nowhere else to go. Thus, the transfer of power into black hands put them in danger of being wiped out altogether. Meanwhile, suspicion arose among ANC activists that Mandela and the government had made a deal behind their backs, a deal that might be inadequate. Some activists found it difficult to give up on equality through revolution in favor of equality through dialogue.

It took two more years of dialogue (and a referendum held among those with the right to vote – that is, white citizens only – in which 70 percent supported the emerging agreement) until the government and the resistance organizations agreed to begin negotiations, and then another two years until they concluded. And all the while, before and during the negotiations, there were crises, breakdowns in talks, and points where the differences seemed too great to bridge. In addition, this final period saw outbreaks of violence even more severe than those of the 1980s. The violence came both from black groups who felt that the pace of progress toward achieving full rights was too slow and that the negotiations might be nothing more than a pretense designed to silence them, and from white extremists who felt that the ground was slipping away from under their feet. And this white violence was committed at times by groups within the security forces, some of them secret sub-organizations established during the time of former President Botha, groups who did everything in their power – including murder – to sabotage what was for them a nightmare unfolding before their eyes.

The challenges of dialogue stemmed not only from opponents of the talks on both sides, terrorist acts by both black and white organizations and individuals, long-standing suspicion between the sides, and threats of civil war or a coup (from both white and black extremists, who suddenly found themselves on the same side of the fence: opposing the approaching compromise). A deep ideological chasm separated the two leaders as well. To be sure, de Klerk's declaration was revolutionary and his actions – including the repeal of the state of emergency and the remaining discriminatory laws, most notably the Population Registration Act, which was the basis for the separation between black, white, and colored – were courageous. But the picture of South Africa he envisioned in no way resembled the one Mandela aspired to. De Klerk was not prepared to accept simple majority rule. Rather, the regime he aimed for would be one of shared, equal rule between groups representing white, colored, and black citizens, divided by tribe, with the weight of each group untethered from the size of the population it represented.

De Klerk walked a tightrope between his interlocutors from the ANC on one side and the extremist branches of his partners in power on the other. More than once, his political conduct, and perhaps also his sincere misgivings, led to crises of trust between him and Mandela. But even in times of crisis, de Klerk remained faithful to his goal: the end of the apartheid regime and the building of a new South Africa. He avoided forceful responses from the security forces at his disposal even when the temperature rose, and treated his rival and interlocutor, Nelson Mandela, with respect.

Over the course of these years of pre-negotiation and actual negotiations, Mandela, for his part, completed a process he began in prison: becoming not just the leader of the struggle for equal rights for black and colored people, but a leader who also knew how to speak to white people about their political views and concerns. He knew that nothing would come of subjugating the white population and denigrating them as a group. He was sensitive to their perception of themselves as native sons of South Africa, and he never denied their right to be an equal part of it. Inevitably, white people were to be partners in the new South Africa he envisioned. Again and again, he emphasized the role played by those white people who struggled alongside black and colored people fighting for equality. In this way, he fostered a readiness for reconciliation among black people. No less important, he offered white people their own heroes with whom they could identify and a narrative of "good" white people to which they could aspire. Mandela understood the white citizens' fear of losing power and spoke of a new South Africa in which all races would be equal. He understood the need for the Afrikaners (Afrikaans-speaking white people – as opposed to English-speaking white people – and those who shaped and led the apartheid regime) to be recognized as native to the continent and deemed their natural connection to the country's soil to be equal to anyone else's. He justified the armed struggle of the Afrikaners against British colonialism in the late nineteenth and early twentieth centuries, thereby honoring Afrikaner pride and asserting that their right to employ violence as a means to secure their own freedom was every bit as legitimate as the right of black and colored people to do the same. Through this gesture, he also provided white people a digestible narrative of this struggle.

Mandela's conduct during one of the lowest points of the negotiations – the murder of a leading activist and member of the Communist Party, by a white racist – was an astonishing expression of his unique empathy and absolute commitment to the process of dialogue with the white regime. More than this, it demonstrated his ability to look into the future and draw his words from the picture he saw there in his mind's eye. In a television broadcast in which he once again addressed the entire nation – that is, all races – as if his leadership were a fait accompli, Mandela spoke about the severity and ugliness of the act and how failed negotiations would place the entire nation on the precipice of bloodshed. But then he shifted his focus to the one who in his eyes was the heroine of the tragic event: a white woman of Afrikaner descent who risked her life to reveal the identity of the white murderer who had tried to thwart any possibility of reaching an agreement. The emphasis that Mandela placed on white people who desired equality would have an impact later on as well. In narratives of the new South Africa, including those that appear in museums dealing with the country's history, a significant role is given to white citizens who were partners in the struggle against apartheid, a greater role than they actually had. This is not the stuff of fabrications; the stories are all true and inspiring. Rather, it's a matter of emphasizing and amplifying their relative weight in a way that is reminiscent of the place occupied by the Warsaw Ghetto Uprising in Jewish and especially Israeli-Jewish Holocaust narratives. After all, most Jews in the Holocaust did not participate in uprisings, but such acts represent what Israeli-Jewish society wants or is willing to identify with.

Despite their crises and disagreements, Mandela and de Klerk were partners in the deepest sense. And even though their conversation began while Mandela was still a prisoner, the two embarked on a journey toward creating a new South Africa with the understanding that their positions carried equal weight and with the knowledge that any solution they reached would have to be acceptable to both. Mandela and de Klerk acted with the understanding that they – like the populations they represented – were interdependent, that their living in the same country was a given, and that neither could bring about change without the other. Above all, the two were driven by an understanding that neither side alone could determine South Africa's future – neither the black majority, who were likely to be the winning side, nor the white minority, who had the power and the governmental, administrative, and economic experience but were destined to be the losing side.

In November 1993, eight years of negotiations – some secret, some public, conducted through many channels and in many places: a hospital, a prison, private homes, and government offices – reached their end. The interim constitution outlining the future South Africa was agreed upon by twenty-six parties and movements, including the Communist Party on the far left and the "Old Guard," the veteran wing of the National Party, on the far right. In a courageous step that was difficult for both of them but underscored their determination, Mandela and de Klerk agreed that if the more extreme factions on each side did not join the agreement, they would sign the constitution without them.

The most difficult issue they faced was the need to reconcile majority rule – which the black side demanded – with rule based on the equality of all ethnic groups – which the white side demanded. The compromise that was reached stated that although the majority would hold most of the power, there would be checks and balances, as well as a form of gradualism. The checks and balances involved significant decentralization of power across nine local governments. Gradualism meant that in the first government, vice presidents were to be drawn from the second and third largest parties, and ministers could come from the minority parties.

There are additional issues in the agreement that are worth dwelling on, because they speak to a larger sensibility at work. These include the "consensus-seeking spirit" clause, which was agreed upon in response to de Klerk's demand that the president would need a two-thirds majority in the cabinet for important decisions. This clause, which emphasizes decency and mutual respect and belongs, in a sense, to the conceptual world of gentlemanly friendship, expressed the spirit of the constitution, a spirit based on both the pragmatism and goodwill of the victorious party, as well as the bureaucratic and economic power of the white population. In addition, a significant portion of the constitution was dedicated to ensuring the security of the white minority, both physically, from acts of revenge, and economically, by securing the jobs and pensions of white police officers, soldiers, and public servants, all of which made them, in practice, partners in the new government. A separate section – the Bill of Fundamental Rights – guaranteed the rights of all citizens of the country. Last, they agreed on a new flag and a new anthem that was a combination of the hymn of the liberation organizations and the Afrikaner anthem.

The agreement they reached was in fact a working draft. It was agreed as well that following the first democratic elections, the two houses of parliament, with their new multiparty and multiracial representation, would draft the final constitution, based on the provisional one, within two years. The constitution, adopted in 1996, is indeed particularly liberal in terms of civil rights and was designed as such to be the antithesis of the apartheid constitution, which had been conservative and restrictive, and at the same time had claimed to represent a democratic state. This would seem to be a contradiction, or perhaps even a paradox, but in a situation where white people alone had rights, this was not a true logical flaw, though it may explain why many white people had difficulty digesting the new political reality.

In the free elections of 1994, what seems obvious today but was unimaginable until then happened: black, white, and colored people stood together in the same lines and voted at the same polling stations, with all votes being equal. Mandela became president, de Klerk one of his vice presidents. At his inauguration, Mandela again addressed all South Africans, saying: "We enter into a covenant that we shall build the society in which all South Africans, both black and white, will be able to walk tall, without any fear in their hearts, assured of their inalienable right to human dignity – a rainbow nation at peace with itself and with the world. . . . Never, never, never again shall it be that this beautiful land will again experience the oppression of one by another and suffer the indignity of being the skunk of the world." Mandela's choice to use "covenant," as opposed to "agreement" or "law," echoes the covenant between God and his people, as well as the one between God and Abraham. The choice of this term added additional, sacred validity to the image of the new South Africa, expressing a religious justification for ending apartheid and seeking reconciliation. This justification also drew from the foundations of Christianity, especially those relating to confession and forgiveness.

Mandela's conciliatory tone was not the stuff of public relations or merely a tactical move aimed at garnering sympathy. Rather, it was the expression of a conciliatory creed that had guided him throughout his life and continued to guide him as president. Even during the years he led an armed struggle, it was clear to him that this violence was being employed to make the government and the world address a problem. But he knew such means would not be able to solve it, since nothing can be built from violence. Mandela constantly stressed the close connection between the end of apartheid and reconciliation. Among his first acts as president were his invitation of the widow of Hendrik Verwoerd, the former prime minister and one of the architects of apartheid, to tea, and a meeting with Percy Yutar, the prosecutor in the trial of Mandela on charges of treason. Yutar had asked the court then to sentence Mandela to death. The Truth and Reconciliation Commission was the embodiment of this conciliatory doctrine.

The commission, officially a state commission of inquiry, was established in 1995 on the basis of the 1993 agreements. It was based on other models of "transitional justice," such as the truth commission established in Chile to investigate the years of Pinochet's dictatorship and the one that investigated the period of military dictatorship in Argentina. The name of the committee reflects the worldview that gave rise to it: revealing the truth is the path to reconciliation. It is worth noting that the name of the commission, which can be understood as the title of the reconciliation process, the thing that justifies and underscores its significance, does not mention achieving justice. This is a matter of great importance, which I will consider more later. The commission's goals were to investigate, document, and denounce the injustices of the apartheid regime, as well as the acts of terrorism committed by the organizations that fought against it. In the eyes of Albie Sachs – a Jewish South African lawyer and professor of law, human rights activist, and anti-apartheid activist – one of the main motivations for establishing the Truth and Reconciliation Commission was the ANC's desire to investigate itself for crimes committed by its members during the years of struggle. According to Sachs – who was persecuted by the apartheid regime and exiled, lost a hand and sight in one eye in an assassination attempt by the apartheid apparatus, and later served as a judge on the Supreme Constitutional Court in the new South Africa – this two-pronged approach made this commission unique throughout the world.

The commission's objectives also included: rehabilitating victims of the apartheid era on both sides, enabling them to have their voices heard, offering them compensation, and assisting in an orderly and peaceful transfer of power, without resentment or revenge. These steps aimed to contribute to national unity and reconciliation in an atmosphere of understanding, one that would transcend past disputes and hardships and thus prevent the recurrence of human rights violations. We must add to these formal goals the enormous and perhaps not always realistic expectations that citizens of the new South Africa had for the commission: justice, mental healing, and physical rehabilitation.

Two sources of moral inspiration informed the commission's founding and operation: ubuntu and Christianity. Ubuntu, "humanity" in Zulu, is an African worldview asserting that a person's humanity stems from the humanity of other people. In everyday life, ubuntu finds its expression in compassion and mutual aid. In the context of reconciliation, it means that when one person harms another, he also harms his own integrity as a human being. When a victim forgives, he restores his attacker's humanity and thus restores his own humanity as well.

The commission drew not only moral validity from Christianity, but also ceremonial symbols and the central principle that guided all its work: forgiveness in exchange for truth. The vast majority of black, colored, and white South Africans are Christians, and this system of concepts and symbols resonated with their faith. Both Mandela and de Klerk emphasized the Christian imperative of forgiveness.

The commission was headed by Desmond Tutu, an Anglican priest and leader in the struggle for equality, as well as an advocate of nonviolent resistance. Though it is hard to believe, Tutu had been appointed by the Anglican Church, headquartered in Britain, to serve as the head of the Anglican Church in South Africa. Thus the black priest was the highest religious authority in the country – even for white believers, even under apartheid rule. Tutu suffused the commission's work with a devout Christian atmosphere. He established the hearings as a purifying and corrective religious experience, similar to the experience of a believer who confesses his sins to a priest, repents, and then receives forgiveness.

The commission was given judicial powers, including the authority to pardon perpetrators of crimes, provided they told the full truth and proved that their crimes were committed within the framework of political ideology and not out of greed or other personal motives. Formally, no one was immune from standing trial: private citizens, members of the old regime and its various branches, and activists of the ANC (whose members were now the ruling party) who had committed murder in their fight against the apartheid regime and against each other, particularly the murders of suspected collaborators with the white government. Appearing before the commission was voluntary, but anyone who had reason to appear – that is, anyone who had something to confess but chose not to – could face criminal trial instead if sufficient evidence was gathered. The commission also had the authority to summon anyone it deemed appropriate to testify before it.

Many ordinary people, including quite a few police officers and soldiers, voluntarily appeared before the commission. However, only a minority of those who bore the most responsibility – the higher-ups who made policy and gave orders – appeared. Despite expectations, the promise of amnesty did not entice such people to face the commission. This may have been because they viewed as empty the threat that they could face criminal trial if they did not appear. After all, these men were well-versed in the legal system and knew how difficult it would be to convict them. Botha, the country's president during the final decade of apartheid rule, is the most famous, glaring case of someone who did not respond to the commission's summons. He refused to appear before what he called a "circus." He was given a fine and a suspended sentence for his refusal, but these were overturned on appeal. As for a criminal trial, prosecutors never assembled the evidence needed to bring charges.

De Klerk, on the other hand, testified before the commission and reiterated his apology for the suffering caused by apartheid, though it is worth noting that his apology was very general and vague. He did not accept personal responsibility, instead acting as if apartheid were something that fell from the sky and not a system driven by people who made decisions and committed acts. De Klerk also insisted that the leaders of the apartheid regime were "good and honorable" people, and that apartheid should neither be viewed as a crime against humanity nor compared to genocide, as some had done. He explained that such a comparison was a surefire recipe for a resurgence of racial tensions. As for his personal responsibility, he remained steadfast in his position that he was unaware of any explicit directives given from the government to the security forces to target black people. Tutu himself presented evidence to the contrary, but de Klerk insisted that neither during his tenure as president nor while serving as a member of the most senior government security forums was he aware of such orders. Tutu was upset by this position. Attempts to get de Klerk to apologize personally to the commission angered many sectors of the white public, and the commission – which had already been accused by these same factions of being one-sided – withdrew.

The commission's proceedings enjoyed a massive following. Newspapers, radio, and television provided extensive coverage. State television broadcasted a daily summary each evening, and a weekly 45-minute program brought viewers voices and images from the deliberations.

The commission received over 21,000 affidavits from those who claimed to have been victims of human rights violations. Ninety percent of these came from black South Africans, mostly women, who in many cases approached the commission on behalf of a dead man to whom they were related – a son, a father, a partner. Public hearings were held at the commission's headquarters in Cape Town, and in various communities as well, in many cases townships, those impoverished ghettos to which the black population had been exiled in order to reserve the cities for white people. These hearings selected and discussed "representative" cases of human rights violations, less than ten percent of all cases brought before the commission. In order to encourage collective introspection, the committee also initiated discussions examining the "softer" and less formal institutional discrimination that prevailed in various sectors of the economy, including academia, banks, the commercial sector, and health care. Judges were the only ones who refused as a group to cooperate with the work of the commission, a refusal many citizens found hard to swallow. Discussions about institutional discrimination reinforced the narrative that there were those who benefited – economically and socially – from apartheid, however indirectly, simply by virtue of being white South Africans.

The issue of beneficiaries remained difficult to digest, as can be seen from an incident that occurred in 2012. Roger Young, a white writer and filmmaker, exhibited black T-shirts with the words "I benefited from apartheid" and offered to sell them "to whites only" in an attempt to shed light on the painful economic reality of the new South Africa. Black people are still discriminated against because they struggle to compete with white people, whose opening conditions when applying for studies and work are better. Of course, all this is a direct result of the preference white people received during the apartheid years, preference that depended in no way on their politics. Simply being white was enough. This incident occurred nearly two decades after the end of apartheid. Nevertheless, the affair sparked great anger among parts of the white public, who were unwilling to accept collective responsibility and felt instead that engaging in such things amounted to pointless self-flagellation.

The commission also received 7,124 affidavits from individuals who sought amnesty for acts they had committed, authorized, or failed to prevent. To be eligible for amnesty, the applicant had to prove that the crime in question was committed as part of a political objective during the conflict and not for personal gain. A request for forgiveness was not a precondition for receiving a pardon, although, as mentioned, the Christian spirit of forgiveness and atonement governed the work of the commission. There were cases in which people asked for forgiveness on their own initiative. In order to receive a pardon, the applicant was required to accept responsibility for his actions, as well as tell the truth about them and the circumstances in which they occurred. This was one of the most remarkable characteristics of the Truth and Reconciliation Commission. Its concept of justice differs from that familiar to us from other justice systems. And it may also differ from most people's intuitive concept of justice. The commission emphasized uncovering the truth as the primary means of doing justice, as opposed to punishing criminals, which is typical of criminal justice systems and was also the case, for example, in the Nuremberg trials.

In October 1998, Desmond Tutu presented President Mandela with the conclusions of the Truth and Reconciliation Commission, bound in five thick volumes. These included a strong condemnation of both sides for the atrocities they committed during the apartheid era; 849 pardons; 20,000 citizens found entitled to financial compensation totaling approximately $40 million, approximately $2,000 each over six years; and the introduction of human rights education into the security system, schools, and universities.

An examination of the achievements of the Truth and Reconciliation Commission should be made in light of its goals and the expectations placed upon it. No less important than what was achieved is what wasn't, either because the commission came up short or because the expectations were unrealistic to begin with. An appraisal of this sort can offer a glimpse into the gap between the ideal of reconciliation and its reality. We can see how such a gap comes to be, sometimes in a painful and upsetting way, and yet this gap is subsumed within the process and does not undermine reconciliation as such.

It is difficult to overstate the importance of some of the commission's achievements. First and foremost, it uncovered the truth. Not the whole truth, but much of it. In fact, exposing the truth was the stated goal and was presented as a necessary condition for reconciliation, as the only basis upon which reconciliation can and must exist. Not justice, not repair. No, these probably belong to the realm of the ideal. Truth.

We still have, of course, the question of what exactly truth is. Perhaps that is why the process of uncovering the "truth" focused on facts. Naturally, the personal, subjective narratives of the victims and the criminals, as individuals and as a collective, also emerged. But the reliance on facts – what deed was done, when it was done, how it was done, and by whom – made it possible to assume that what was revealed was objective truth, and I use those words together with great caution and with all the necessary reservations.

Indeed, reservation is called for. As I said, much of the truth was revealed, not the whole truth. The commission exposed blatant human rights violations, the mechanism behind them, and the apartheid culture that enabled them, but many felt that not enough emphasis was given to the "big picture," to the political and state structures that constituted the apartheid regime. The question stands regarding whether it is even possible to paint such a picture. It seems to me likely that a certain gap between what was experienced under tyranny and the ability to describe it will always exist. There is a basis for this complaint, however, one based on the understandable frustration at the refusal of senior apartheid officials to accept responsibility. The commission thus painted a detailed picture of the experiences of the victims and the guilt of the perpetrators at the lower and middle levels, but a very incomplete, even implicit, picture of the higher levels. Many parts of South African society were left with a bad taste in their mouths. The lion's share of the senior figures in the apartheid regime paid no price for what they had done, unless – and there may be something to this – their loss of the power and the refutation of the narrative that allowed them to maintain this power are to be seen as a price of some sort.

Another achievement of the commission, which was a result of its focus on uncovering the truth, was the opportunity it gave victims to make their voices heard in an official forum where they were publicly recognized, and with all that this opportunity implies and entails. This wasn't just a matter of giving legitimacy to voices that had been silenced under apartheid. Such a process fundamentally changed something in their power relations with those who had violated their most basic rights. The victims not only spoke about what had happened to them; the commission allowed them and encouraged them to be active in relation to the perpetrators of the crime: to ask, to demand, to interrogate, to cast doubt. In many cases, victims asked the perpetrators of a crime for details about the incident – *why* they did what they did, what was the *context* in which they did what they did, *how* they did what they did, what the perpetrators were *thinking*, and how the whole *system* worked: *from whom* they received the instruction or *to whom* they gave it, and how *exactly* it worked. Hidden graves were revealed, as were the fates of many who were disappeared by the security forces during the apartheid era. Through this process of extracting knowledge from those who were part of the apartheid regime and making it public, the victims effectively took ownership of history.

Thanks to this challenging testimony, sometimes accompanied by outbursts of powerful emotion from both victims and listeners, the contours of the past emerged with undeniable clarity. In this way, the commission added to the collective historical narrative of the underlying social and governmental culture within which these human rights violations occurred. In effect, the commission transformed apartheid from a nameless, faceless system that existed simply because it existed, much like the weather, into a system that was built, maintained, and operated by real people with names and faces, people who committed crimes for the sake of this system. In doing so, the commission fulfilled a request made by the nineteen-year-old daughter of a murdered anti-apartheid activist: "We want to forgive, but we don't know who." This request echoes the understanding that while reconciliation occurs between groups, forgiveness is an interpersonal act that requires an actual human being who embodies an injustice.

There is another side to uncovering the truth, no less significant and every bit as complex. Just as uncovering the truth and giving a name and a face to the culture of apartheid restored black citizens' right to know, this process also took away from white people their right not to know. Many white people took great advantage of this right; indeed, large parts of this population continued trying to hold on to it in the post-apartheid era as well. De Klerk was the clearest, most prominent example of someone who claimed – outrageously – to be unaware of the atrocities committed by and in the name of the regime he headed. Too many made this disturbing, outrageous claim: I had no part in the system, I had nothing to do with apartheid. But this was impossible, for if no one got their hands dirty, how could this regime have persisted and how could this machinery of repression have functioned? By exposing the full extent of human rights violations, the commission also refuted a claim made by many white people: only a small number of people perpetrated these awful crimes. A few bad apples. The larger white population insisted that the wrongs these individuals committed did not sully the community to which they belonged, and in whose name they acted.

It is not difficult to understand the motivation behind this white denial. From the moment the apartheid regime started to crumble and its horrors began to emerge, disturbing questions arose about how exactly it could have been possible in the first place. There seems to be no limit to the powers of human denial. This mechanism was not invented in white South Africa during the years of apartheid. It is familiar from other periods in history – both recent and not – and from other places in the world – both distant and near – but it is stunning to witness it all the same. How and in the name of what could most white people in the country have been convinced to support an oppressive, racist regime? How could they have been convinced that it was impossible to talk with black people? How could they have been convinced to ignore the townships to which black people were exiled, where they lived in abject conditions? How could they have been convinced that the country's violence stemmed from black people's violent nature and that force was the only answer to this violence – and when that didn't work, the only answer was more force? How could they think and do all this while continuing, at the very same time, to see themselves as members of a democratic society?

But uncovering the truth came at a cost. The commission heard thousands of testimonies, many of them heartbreaking. Many tears were shed as the victims told their stories and the criminals confessed their crimes. Tutu himself cried a lot, and there were times when the courtroom went silent and the hearing stopped until he could pull himself together. The details were often graphic. Victims relived the horrors, as happened, for example, in the case where mothers of murdered victims collapsed when they were "privileged" to see, a decade after the fact, a video documenting the murder of their children. An event such as this revealed a flaw in the commission's work.

After the knowledge of a crime was disclosed, after the criminal accepted responsibility, and after the establishment officially recognized the victim, these same victims were left to deal with their trauma. No treatment or rehabilitation mechanism was established for them. This weakness of the commission stemmed from objective limitations: it operated within a limited time frame, with limited manpower, and with a limited budget. But there were subjective limitations as well. Enormous, sometimes unrealistic, expectations were placed on it: that it would enable healing on an individual and not just a collective basis; that it would function like a parent who takes care of their child's most basic needs.

Bringing the truth to light also exposed what the commission did not achieve. Many of those involved were left with the feeling that they hadn't reached the end of their story, that they were part of a dialogue that was interrupted and thus incomplete, and that they were left "with their tongues hanging out." Indeed, the natural human reaction to the presence of injustice is: What now? Will someone be punished? Will someone be compensated? How can we move on to present concerns? In other words: Where is the justice?

It is at this point that the following question, with all its gravity, must be posed: What exactly is the relationship between reconciliation and justice? Or, more precisely: Is justice a necessary or even possible component of reconciliation? Tutu's answer was unequivocal: "If justice alone is done, the country will turn to ashes." In practice, the commission limited the definition of justice in order to arrive at a working concept: justice is achieved by revealing the truth. This is a narrow definition of justice, or perhaps a definition of the kind of justice that can be achieved and, therefore, the kind that cannot. At this point, the tension between the individual and the collective emerges once again. This tension reveals the conflict, and sometimes even the contradiction, between reconciliation and justice, as well as the unequivocal choice that was made in the South

African case. Reconciliation was chosen, and many aspects of what is traditionally and perhaps naturally perceived as justice – certainly at the level of the individual – were sacrificed.

A clear example of this was the decision to deny survivors the right to sue in civil or criminal court those who committed crimes against them and were granted amnesty by the commission. This is a basic, constitutional right that belongs to any person in a democratic society like the new South Africa – the right to demand compensation from those who committed crimes against them. However, in this reconciliation process, deliberations about past crimes were transferred to a non-criminal framework. This move prioritized the healing of the community over the possibility of the individual seeing their perpetrator pay a personal price for his crimes.

Or at the very least, apologize. Here, too, a painful compromise was made, one that shows the difference between this reconciliation process and what is traditionally and perhaps naturally perceived as justice: those who committed a crime were required to tell the truth and accept responsibility, but they were not required to apologize. There were, to be sure, instances where criminals apologized and repented profoundly and publicly for their sins. But there were also painful and outrageous cases where people told the truth and accepted responsibility, but did so with a crooked, telling smile, that of a villain who has managed to escape punishment.

Another aspect of justice was sacrificed on the altar of reconciliation: repair. This, too, is deeply embedded in our perception of justice: much like we are accustomed to thinking that crime requires punishment, so too are we accustomed to thinking that wrongdoing requires repair. And yet, in this regard, the reconciliation process made a clear choice: South Africa was to look to the future, not the past. In order to do this, the recognition of past wrongs was severed from the concrete follow-up such recognition would seem to demand: the redress of these wrongs. In fact, South Africa's reconciliation process has made clear what is often difficult to accept: the past cannot be undone, repair can only be made in relation to the future.

For example, those whose parents or grandparents were expelled from their homes in the cities to the townships during the apartheid era were unable to return to them in the new South Africa, in which there were no longer legal restrictions on where they could live. The places from which black people were expelled were now populated by white people who viewed these places as their home. The simple rule that one cannot correct an injustice by committing a new injustice is at work here. In this case, one does not evict a person from his home in order to return that home to someone who was previously evicted from it. Even so, it is not difficult to see how outrageous this is. Through A – an energetic, open woman in her thirties with whom I worked in Cape Town – I became acquainted with the bitterness that is often the lot of those who experience the dissonance between living in a society that has been reformed, at least on paper, and the ongoing injustice in their daily lives. On one of our trips, she asked the driver to slow down and pointed to a beautiful, well-maintained house perched on top of a hill. "That was ours," she said, and for a moment her nostrils flared with suppressed fury. "Sometimes my grandmother asks me to bring her here." The grandmother, a black woman from Cape Town, married a half-Japanese, half-white man who came to South Africa for business. They lived in the house that A pointed out, on a beautiful, green hill with a breathtaking view. But back in those days, oppressive, discriminatory legislation was deepened and expanded. The couple was forced to live according to society's definitions: it was unthinkable (to the white mind) that a colored man married to a black woman would be allowed to live in the city. The grandmother – along with her children, grandchildren, and great-grandchildren – still lives in the poor neighborhood to which they were expelled. And so, from time to time, she asks someone in the family to drive her to the old neighborhood, where she sits in the car and looks out at the house in silence.

The example undermines our sense of justice in an additional way: equal opportunity, or the lack thereof. In concrete terms, it was not practically possible for this family, or any other, to return to the home from which they were evicted. For even if the home were vacant, years of systematic oppression and discrimination left them poor and, for the most part, uneducated and lacking the tools to bring about a change in their situation. In this case, the rule that you can't fix one injustice by causing another does not apply. It's about major objective limits on money and time. Money, by nature, always has a limit. Time, by nature, is indifferent to human will. Even given these resources, it would take years, generations perhaps, to improve the economic and social situation of those who were oppressed by the apartheid regime and whose economic and human resources were depleted as a result. The gap between achieving political rights and enjoying a life of basic dignity – the latter was often not realized – is often very difficult to digest.

Finally, another important question (which is of even greater importance in the Rwandan case, as we will soon see) addresses the element of free choice that South Africans did or did not have in the reconciliation process. In other words: to what extent were South Africans allowed to choose whether to reconcile or not? Formally, they had a choice. The reconciliation process was led by a democratically elected government, and the Truth and Reconciliation Commission was attended by those choosing to participate – certainly from among the victims and, to a meaningful extent, from among those who had violated their human rights. Yet in a way, the reconciliation process was like a wave in the ocean: you could swim toward it and dive into it, or you could wait for it to reach you. But you couldn't remain in the ocean that was South Africa without that wave hitting you. It was hard to be a South African in those years and remain indifferent to the reconciliation process. It was everywhere. The media amplified it, and it was the main focus of public discourse. The reconciliation process was also driven by the feeling that without it, South Africans might find themselves in a bloodbath. President Mandela and Desmond Tutu threw their full political and moral weight into creating a climate of reconciliation. The overlap between reconciliation and Christian values of forgiveness that the two leaders promoted resonated with most South Africans. A good Christian came to be seen as a Christian who reconciles, that is, one who asks for forgiveness or forgives. And who doesn't want to see themselves as a good Christian? The climate of reconciliation created social pressure to reconcile. This pressure probably reduced the freedom of the individual, who may not always have felt comfortable forgiving. This pressure was difficult to resist, and Desmond Tutu applied it with determination. He also often initiated dramatic gestures of reconciliation, coaxing the victim and the aggressor to verbally suggest reconciliation – to confess a sin, to ask for forgiveness, to say explicitly, "I forgive you." People were even encouraged to perform concrete, physical gestures of reconciliation – to stand up, to reach out, to hug. In this regard, the political and religious leadership's designation of reconciliation as a goal preceded the ability of most people to reconcile and marked the way for them. To be precise: this was not one of several options offered to South Africans by their leaders; it was the only option. The individual had the freedom to choose how far he would go and at what pace, not whether he would participate at all.

The case of Winnie Mandela, perhaps the most famous and dramatic of all those discussed by the commission, demonstrates both the artificial and coercive elements of the reconciliation process. Not only this, her case illustrates the complexity and difficulty of deciding moral questions, of establishing who is "good" and who is "bad," even in South Africa, where this dichotomy was supposedly straightforward. Winnie Mandela was a symbol of the struggle against apartheid, as the wife of Nelson Mandela, as a leader in the ANC's struggle for equality in general, and as a leader of ANC women in particular. She was nicknamed "Mother of the Nation." She was loud and bold, her actions uniquely colored by her theatrical personality, which was very different from that of Nelson Mandela – who was restrained and measured, the one who was seen as the "responsible adult." The couple separated two years after Nelson Mandela was released from prison, and they divorced four years later.

During the years of struggle, Winnie Mandela took a tough and violent line, not just against white people but also against those black people whom she suspected of collaborating. Some understood her extreme positions – including her call for the use of "necklace killing," an execution method in which a person is murdered by placing a burning tire around his neck – as a response to the persecution of the apartheid regime and the horrific torture she endured while in prison for her activism. Whatever the case, she did not speak the language of reconciliation, but that of struggle and triumph, and she didn't change during the years of negotiations with the government. In the violence-filled 1980s, she founded the United Mandela Football Club, a group of young people who organized themselves around her and, despite its name, played very little football, if any. Its members were presented as her bodyguards, but in reality displayed a cult-like loyalty and willingness to employ violence at her command.

Before the Truth and Reconciliation Commission, Mandela claimed that the eighteen human rights violations she was accused of, including eight murders, were "ridiculous." She was nevertheless found guilty (in a 1991 criminal trial and then later at the 1998 Truth and Reconciliation Commission) of, among other things, the kidnapping and abuse of four black youth whom she suspected of collaborating with the apartheid regime's security forces. She was also found guilty of the diluted charge of "negligence" that led to the death of one of them, Stompy. The four boys were in a Methodist church under the care of Reverend Paul Verryn, a white man who worked for equal rights and had gained the sympathy and trust of the black population in the Soweto Township, where he worked. Verryn provided protection to the four anti-apartheid activists, as he did for other young men being pursued by the security forces. But these four were abducted from there by Mandela's men and brought to her house, where they were tortured by her and her men. One of the boys, Stompy Moeketsi, a fourteen-year-old who had been an anti-apartheid activist since the age of ten, was murdered, his body found in a Soweto dump.

One of the leaders of the "football club," the one who killed Stompy, was convicted of the murder. Before the Truth and Reconciliation Commission, the accused testified that Winnie Mandela herself had given him the murder weapon, and that he had murdered the boy on the orders of "Mummy," as she was affectionately known by many. Joyce, Stompy's mother, testified before the commission and attended its deliberations. The expression on her large, round face hardly ever changed, as if she were frozen in pain. Quiet, sometimes sobbing softly, she sat in the audience, facing the witnesses and Mandela, and heard horrific descriptions of the torture her son endured in his final days under Mandela's control. This testimony included graphic descriptions of how two of her "bodyguards" repeatedly threw the boy in the air, knocked him down, and kicked him like he was a football, all while Winnie Mandela stood next to them and watched. When the killer told how he had slaughtered the teen like a goat, accompanying his words with demonstrative gestures of his hands and neck, the mother stood up and left the hall, still silent.

The Stompy affair, which became a symbol of apartheid's atrocities, is just one of the cases raised by the commission concerning blatant human rights violations for which Winnie Mandela was directly or indirectly responsible. This affair was also much more branched and complicated than this summary might suggest. Its twists and turns destroyed many more lives. To justify the kidnapping of the boys from the church where they were hiding from security forces, Mandela claimed that Reverend Paul Verryn – a harsh critic of Mandela, her group, and her methods – had raped them. At the commission's hearings, those who had testified against him in the criminal trial held a few years earlier, including his black housekeeper, said that they had lied. According to them, they had been coerced into doing so by Mandela's people, who operated using such forceful and manipulative means that it was difficult and even dangerous not to comply with them.

Eight years later, the commission cleared Verryn of all wrongdoing. In his testimony, Verryn turned to Mandela, who listened impassively and did not respond, and said: "I long for reconciliation between us. . . . I have struggled to reach a place of forgiveness, even if you do not *want* my forgiveness, or even don't think I *deserve* to offer you my forgiveness." By emphasizing the words "want" and "deserve," Verryn expressed his awareness of what, in Mandela's eyes, was perhaps absurd: a white person forgives a black person even as the "greater" guilt would always lie with the white person.

Another branch of the Stompy affair concerns Dr. Abu Baker Asvat, a community doctor and human rights activist of Asian origin. Asvat was a friend and the doctor of the Mandela family. Despite this, he refused to comply with her request that he declare that the kidnapped boys being held in her home had been raped by Verryn. Two days later, as Stompy lay dying in her home, Mandela asked Asvat to examine him. Asvat did as he was asked, and after examining him, he told her that Stompy's injuries were critical, that his life was in danger, and that his condition required immediate evacuation to a hospital. But Mandela chose not to listen to his recommendation. Asvat was murdered in his clinic a few weeks later.

Mandela initially tried to shift the blame for the murder onto Pastor Verryn, claiming that Asvat knew he had raped the boys and could therefore testify to this and convict Verryn. Later, Mandela herself was accused of having her men murder Asvat, who could testify about both her attempt to shift the blame for the rape onto Verryn as well as Stompy's condition while he was being held in her home and under her responsibility. Asvat's family begged for information about the events leading up to his death. Asvat's brother sat through the commission's hearings, weeping. But there was not enough evidence to convict Mandela, and the question of who was responsible for his murder remains unanswered.

Throughout the hearings, Mandela remained confident and calm, almost indifferent. Occasionally a faint, disdainful smile passed across her face, but for the most part she remained serious, attentive, and firm in her account, even when it was refuted, witness after witness. She repeatedly denied everything she was accused of and refused to accept any responsibility. Desmond Tutu had been forced to warn her during the period when they were discussing the Stompy case to order her people to stop threatening Joyce, his mother, in an attempt to influence her testimony. At the end of the hearings, Tutu personally addressed Mandela with great emotion. He cloaked his remarks in a larger appreciation for Mandela, their long friendship, and his deep love for her. Tutu told her that many people longed to forgive her but could do so only if she would find a way to admit something, even something general, even a statement like "Things went horribly wrong and I'm sorry they went terribly wrong." He presented his words to her in a way he thought she could accept, and pleaded with her. He had left Mandela with no choice. She had to offer something to the commission.

After consulting with her lawyers, she did echo Tutu's words and offered a nonbinding expression of regret: "I would like to take this opportunity to tell Dr. Asvat's family how deeply sorry I am and to Stompy's mother how deeply sorry I am . . . and I say it's true: things went horribly wrong. I agree with that and for that part of those painful years when things went horribly wrong and we were aware that there were factors that led to that. For that I am deeply sorry."

The Winnie Mandela case demonstrates the complexity of South Africa during apartheid and the difficulty of doing justice in the simplest sense: Even in a "black and white" situation, where it is ostensibly clear who is "good" and who is "bad," how do we decide who the victim is? And how do we decide to what extent victimhood can justify actions that would otherwise be unacceptable? Peter Storey – a white Methodist minister and human rights activist who eulogized Stompy at his funeral and was the chaplain for political prisoners, including Nelson Mandela, at Robben Island – put it well in his testimony before the commission: "The primary cancer [of South Africa] may be, and was, and will always be, the apartheid oppression, but secondary infections have touched many of apartheid's opponents and eroded their knowledge of good and evil."

Rwanda: When Black Is Not Entirely Black and White Is Not Entirely White

It was dark and quiet when I landed at the small, almost neighborhood-like Kigali airport, passed the temperature check imposed during the anxious Ebola era, and met my host, H, a stocky man in his fifties with whom I would work during my stay. There was a fierce expression on his round face, but he was otherwise reserved, a confusing and intriguing – not to mention unsettling – mixture that hinted at what I didn't yet know about the restrained atmosphere that pervades everything in Rwanda. It's a place where people speak in sentences that end with three periods instead of one. There is so much here that cannot be said – because it's forbidden, because it's difficult, because there are no words.

"What time is it?" I asked him.

He looked at his watch and answered, "Half past midnight."

A tall, thin man in Western pants and shoes and an African shirt was standing not far from us and apparently assumed that my question was directed at him. He, too, looked at his watch and answered, "Half past one."

I looked from one to the other, expecting them to come to some sort of agreement, but it seemed that they weren't even considering the option. My host and I said goodbye to the man and left, and I then recalled one of the conversations I had had before my departure, in preparation for this visit. I was told that ethnic differences in Rwanda are swept under the rug. It's a subject that shouldn't be broached. So, as the city's sights passed me by in the car, I wondered whether that was true of all the differences here. Perhaps every dispute has the potential to bring to the surface buried ethnic tensions. And inscribed on the tombstone at this burial: *In order for us not to once again find ourselves in the darkest regions imaginable, every sign of disagreement must be erased.*

Yes, there are many topics that one is forbidden to touch. An uneasy caution surrounds interpersonal communication, especially when it touches on the past or even approaches it, or on ethnic affiliations, or on the government in general and its leader in particular. In fact, for the most part, these exchanges don't at all meet the definition of interpersonal communication, at least as I am accustomed to thinking of it. They're more akin to the almost automatic recitation of the choir I mentioned earlier. When it comes to the past, the voice of the choir sounds something like this: It happened, there were victims and there were victimizers, but now we are all one people facing the future. In regard to ethnic affiliations, the choir's voice is resounding in its silence. After all, using the words "Hutu" and "Tutsi" in public is prohibited by law, despite the fact that everyone knows – based on appearance or simple familiarity – who is Hutu and who is Tutsi. As for the government and its leader, the choir praises the achievements of reconstruction and the booming economy (at least in African terms), the very advanced gender equality, while official photos of the president adorn every public institution and many private ones as well.

A television screen raised on a pole in the center of Kigali, the kind of screen that back home displays ads, shows a looping promotional video of iconic human rights heroes: Mahatma Gandhi, Nelson Mandela, Mother Teresa, and then, of course,

Rwandan President Paul Kagame. Following his image, in large letters spoon-feeding the word to whoever happens to be looking: VISION. A trait common to all four, of course. Under the guise of preventing what the regime calls "ethnic divisionism," parties organized according to ethnic affiliation, such as Hutu, are prohibited. In fact, this is a country where there is only one party with any influence. Political opponents who overly criticize the regime and its leader may find themselves detained, accused of ethnic divisionism or, worse, of "negationism," which in the Rwandan context refers to anything that challenges the official narrative of the genocide.

Kagame himself draws parallels between this law and laws against Holocaust denial that exist in many Western countries. However, for the most part, those who disagree with the official Rwandan narrative do not deny the genocide but seek to direct the spotlight at the fact that it was the culmination of a civil war in which both sides took part. Therefore, in their view, the victim-victimizer dichotomy cannot so simply be applied to the Rwandan case. Reports of physical injuries and political assassinations have found their way out of the country but are strongly denied by the government.

Ordinary Rwandan citizens must also be careful. Anyone who criticizes the regime or the president – in public or on the phone (which the government listens to) – will not be disappeared. But they risk being blacklisted by the ruling party, which in fact controls virtually all aspects of an individual's life, including work. In a country where unemployment stands at 40 percent, most people are in no hurry to jeopardize their source of income. Self-censorship is one of the more depressing signs of such regimes, and it permeates everything. A few days into my second visit to Rwanda, the water in the hostel where I was staying ran out. A thin, short-lived trickle of water could be extracted every few hours from some of the taps and fountains. But in most cases: nothing. The explanation for this, an explanation I heard everywhere and in the exact same words, was that the rainy season was late and therefore the water reservoirs, many of which are filled by rain, had dried up. On the third day without water, I learned from an agronomist I worked with in another neighborhood that they had not had water for two weeks. "The rainy season is late," he told me. And though I searched, I couldn't detect any resentment in him. Along the roadsides, women, men, and children walked for miles to fill buckets from a neighborhood pump and bring them home. No one seemed upset that there were areas in Kigali where the water continued to flow. It's true that there was not much water during this season, but it was there. The government regulates its flow so that the more affluent neighborhood – the one where government officials and foreigners live and where the hotels intended for tourists are located – will (almost) always have water. Questioning the decisions of government officials regarding the regulation of water may be viewed negatively.

Journalists, including foreign ones, also must exercise caution. If they don't, they receive a courtesy reminder from the government – an arrest or the kind of reminder that G, a young British journalist, received when a stone was thrown through her window. This reminder – which followed a series of similar and seemingly accidental reminders – achieved the intended effect with this particular journalist, and she left journalism for philanthropic work in Kigali. The overwhelming number of armed soldiers and police stationed everywhere in the country is a constant reminder of the intrusive and inescapable presence of the government and its agents.

However, the government – its leader especially – enjoys a considerable degree of tolerance, not to mention admiration. This is the case both at home (where it is perhaps possible to argue that the absence of a democratic tradition is one of the reasons) and (for the most part) abroad (where this argument does not hold up). The condition of the country when Kagame accepted, or more precisely, took power, may explain some of the tolerance – and perhaps even submission – with which his rule has been received.

Unadulterated evil, rampaging violence, a social fabric in tatters. The terror was so shocking that even today it operates as an engine that sustains both reconciliation and the regime. The latter has managed to position itself as responsible for reconciliation, for the robustness of this process, and by implication a necessary condition for its very existence. Kagame speaks fluent "Western," but presents himself as an independent who is often critical of the West. And when Western criticism is directed at him, he often shrugs it off. At home he is viewed as a Rwandan patriot who brought about the recovery of a nation that had torn itself apart. He is seen as marching the country toward progress, with the goals he sets the stuff of common sense, even among his opponents: reducing poverty and malnutrition, strengthening the education and health care systems, establishing physical, technological, and economic infrastructure, and above all, national reconciliation. Therein lies his strength.

The following image may perhaps help one understand something of the delusional, even disturbed, state of mind that one experiences as one delves deeper into the Rwandan genocide and the subsequent reconciliation process. In April 2014, an official ceremony to mark the twentieth anniversary of the genocide was held at the Amahoro Stadium in Kigali. Local and international dignitaries spoke about the achievement of reconciliation, along with the reconstruction and prosperity that followed, and performers reenacted events from the massacre in artistic, dramatic fashion. Meanwhile, one by one, people in the audience collapsed and were evacuated to a treatment tent near the stadium that had been set up for this purpose in advance. These cries of dismay and this parade of unconscious people accompanied the sights and sounds of the ceremony, which continued as planned. Those on stage and in the audience transformed into a living, bloody image of Rwandan society. Its reconciliation was distilled down to its almost grotesque essence, something at once stunning in its achievements and disturbing in its costs. In order to try to understand all this, one must revisit the genocide itself, which was unique in that it involved both an institutional aspect – which was planned, systematic, and organized – and a popular aspect – which saw the active participation of "ordinary" Hutus in what seemed like a mass psychosis. Their reconciliation process, and their contemporary reality in general, echoes this uniqueness.

The ethnic groups that make up the population of Rwanda – Hutu, Tutsi, and the tiny Twa minority – share a language, culture, and political framework that, unlike most countries on the continent, also existed in the precolonial era. Although each group had distinguishing external characteristics, the division between them was based on class, not ethnicity. The Hutus were the farmers, while the Tutsis owned the land and the cattle. But it was possible to move between classes: a Hutu who owned many cows became a Tutsi, a Tutsi who lost his cows became Hutu. The colonial regime (the Germans, and later – and more adamantly – the Belgians) introduced a racial theory to the country resembling the one that would wreak havoc in Europe in the years to come. The Germans categorized the groups according to skin color, height, and facial features (in the name of order and accuracy, they measured the thickness of the lips, the circumference of the head, and the width of the nose). The Tutsi – with their lighter skin, "whiter" facial features, and taller stature – were deemed superior to the Hutu (and Twa) – whose darker skin, more "African" features, and shorter stature made them inferior in the same way in which the Germans would later deem Aryans superior to Slavic, Asian, black, Romani, and Jewish people.

Under the Germans, traditional class divisions were transformed into rigid ethnic divisions, across which no one could move. The Germans favored the Tutsi, and although they were a minority (14 percent), they were appointed to most of the key positions in the government and administration. The

Belgians picked up where the Germans left off. Not only did they favor the Tutsi over the Hutu, but they also introduced forced labor that exploited the local population, especially the Hutu, in a way that deepened the separation between the groups and sowed the seeds of jealousy and hatred. And they gave additional legality to this separation, by requiring ethnic registration on identity cards.

The balance of power in the country changed, however, when the Tutsi began to demand independence. In response, the Belgians, starting in 1959, gradually shifted their support to the Hutu. By the time Rwanda gained its independence, in 1962, the Hutu – who, at 85 percent of the population, were the clear majority – already controlled the country's institutions. The Hutus' dictatorial rule emerged after long years of frustration. They had suffered discrimination and exclusion, so the government worked to push Tutsis out of positions of influence. In addition to restrictive legislation, organized riots "erupted" from time to time, in which many Tutsis were murdered, and many more were exiled or fled to neighboring countries. Tutsis who sought to return to their homeland were refused. Sometimes they were allowed to visit their families who stayed behind, but sometimes not.

The Rwandan Patriotic Front (RPF), formed by Tutsi refugees in neighboring countries, waged an armed guerrilla struggle against the government. Struggles between Hutu and Tutsi, with violent outbursts on both sides, broke out in these neighboring countries as well, leading to a decades-long conflict of varying intensity.

The RPF's 1990 invasion into the country is generally considered to mark the start of Rwanda's civil war. The Hutu government exploited the invasion to increase incitement against those Tutsis who remained in Rwanda and allegedly joined forces with the RPF to seize power, kill the Hutu, and expel them from the country. Amid this whirlwind of incitement, the Hutu government raised the question at the very center of every such conflict: Who does this land belong to? The Tutsi were portrayed as foreign invaders. This portrayal played on a historical ambiguity – in the absence of written documentation – as to the exact origin of the Tutsi. Had they come from East Africa, Ethiopia for example, with whose population they share a physical resemblance, or did they evolve as a distinct group from the Hutu, whose ancestors had arrived earlier?

At the same time, the government began making practical preparations for genocide. These preparations, which lasted four years, included, among other things, importing large quantities of weapons (including about half a million machetes) and having people from within the government distribute them to the Hutu masses. Lists of those to be slaughtered were prepared and distributed among key figures, who began to organize and train militias throughout the country. Dedicated media outlets were established, in particular RTLM – the "Free Radio and Television of a Thousand Hills" (as the small, hill-dotted country is known) – to broadcast incitement against the Tutsi masses. These outlets called on Hutus to be vigilant and beware of the Tutsis, who were supposedly threatening to take their land, their cattle, and their lives. Programs about the need for a "final solution" to the "Tutsi problem" were broadcast. Similarities to the wildly racist incitement of Nazi Germany against the Jews did not end with this identical terminology. Nor did it end with legislation marking each person according to their origin, or the "Ten Hutu Commandments," which included, among other things, a ban on "mixed" marriages. In addition, the nickname "cockroaches" was attached to the Tutsi to denote their essence as repulsive creatures who threaten to invade homes through the narrowest cracks. As for what should be done with them, the implication was clear: crush them without thinking too much about it, and with the same ease with which one crushes an insect.

Systematic incitement and preparations for the massacre – preparations that were discussed at government meetings as well as at the local level among mayors and senior police and military officials – took place amidst international pressure. This pressure led the government and the RPF to sign the Arusha Accords, which were designed to end the civil war and bring the country closer to democratization. However, on April 6, 1994, a plane carrying the presidents of Rwanda and Burundi was shot down on its way back from Dar es Salaam, Tanzania, where they, along with the presidents of Tanzania and Uganda and the vice president of Kenya, were participating in a regional conference on the implementation of the Arusha Accords. Both presidents were killed. It was not clear who was responsible for shooting down the plane. Was it Tutsi fighters or Hutu extremists, led by the president's wife, who tried to thwart his position, which was too conciliatory for their liking? Whatever the case, the accusations were directed at the Tutsi.

The establishment, the official media, led by the radio station RTLM, and the local leadership all called on ordinary citizens to murder Tutsis in revenge for the assassination of the president. This call fell on the attentive ears of those who had long been brainwashed with hatred and fear of Tutsis. They were now "ripe" to act.

"Rise and do your work," was broadcast over the radio. The meaning of this seemingly innocent language was well understood. "Cut the tall grass," the call rang out, and it was understood that the reference was not to grass but to the tall, thin Tutsi. The slaughter began simultaneously across the country. Moderate Hutus, including the prime minister and the foreign minister, both of whom supported the Arusha Accords, were also executed. The country's borders were closed and roadblocks set up, making it difficult for the Tutsis to escape. The murderous mob (it's estimated that some 300,000 people took part in the genocide) used mostly simple weapons – machetes and spiked sticks. Military and police personnel also used firearms (some of which were of Israeli origin).

Streets, fields, and public buildings filled with corpses, puddles of blood, and severed limbs. In denser areas, the corpses, so close together it was difficult to distinguish where one ended and the next began, extended in every direction. Piles of bodies thrown into rivers turned into dams that stopped their flow, and those that were dumped into lakes turned their waters red. People were murdered individually – by their neighbors, friends, and sometimes family members – and en masse – in churches by their pastors, for example, or in public buildings to which they had fled in order to hide. And throughout, the media, led by RTLM, continued to egg on the masses: "You have not caught all of our enemies – some of them are still alive," and, "The graves are not yet full – the good work must continue until all of them are filled." This is how the killing machine simultaneously operated from above and below, crushing the Tutsis in the middle. The unimaginable efficiency of the genocide – about 10,000 people per day – was a result of both the preparations made in the years leading up to the massacre and the unique fabric of life in Rwandan society, where Hutu and Tutsi lived side by side and shared streets, neighborhoods, markets, schools, workplaces, and churches. When the order to murder was given, every Hutu knew which of his neighbors, friends, colleagues, or even family members was a Tutsi. The murdered were known well, and often close enough to touch.

The human and physical landscape of the country were altered beyond recognition. Between 800,000 and over a million people were murdered. The vast majority of them were Tutsi, but as I noted earlier, many Hutus were killed as well, either by Hutu militias for not agreeing to take part in the massacre or by Tutsi militias in revenge operations. The estimates of Hutu victims range from tens of thousands to 200,000. About half a million women and girls were victims of rape, in many cases mass rape, which at times included intentional HIV infection. Women's intimate parts were mutilated or amputated and sometimes publicly displayed. Yes, bloody pieces of flesh that were one woman's breast or another woman's genitals were hung on fences and posts. The scope and systematic nature of the rape compelled the international community to recognize rape as a war crime for the first time. Twenty thousand children were born as a result of these rapes. Estimates as to the number of orphans left behind by the slaughter vary from 100,000 to 400,000. The reason for this range is, among other things, the question of whether or not to include those children who were orphaned in the years after the massacre as a result of it. Many children became orphans later on when their parents died of their injuries or their mothers died from AIDS after being infected via rape. Eighty-five thousand orphaned children became heads of their families. One can get a sense of the mental scars carried by the surviving children by studying UNICEF data, which found that 80 percent of Rwandan children experienced the death of a close family member, 70 percent saw someone murdered or injured, and 90 percent believed they themselves were in immediate danger and were likely be killed in a massacre.

And again, to understand the intensity of the fracture, one must remember that the victimizers and the victims were acquaintances from work, school, or church; they were neighbors and friends, and, in cases of "mixed" marriages, there were those who murdered their Tutsi family members. Such a loss of trust is hard to imagine.

H, the colleague who met me at the airport, worked with me closely during my two visits to Rwanda. Once H and his wife, M, invited me to their home for a festive traditional Rwandan meal that included goat meat cooked in tomato paste and cassava, whose green leaves are reminiscent of spinach, while its root reminds one of a potato. They are Hutu. No one said so, of course, but it was clear. After a few days in Rwanda, you learn to identify who is who. We looked at a family photo album together. M wanted to show me their four children, the older ones are studying at universities abroad, the younger ones are at boarding schools. "These people, many of them are no longer alive," M told me quietly, pointing to a photo from some social event, a birthday of one of the men or women in their twenties smiling together at the camera. "It's so terrible," she muttered, "I try to forget." Where H and M were during the genocide, and what they did or didn't do, I don't know. "We were . . . here," she replied to my cautious question in a broken voice, closed the photo album, and got up to clear the plates.

A few days earlier, M had accompanied me, at her husband's request, on my first visit to the Kigali Genocide Memorial museum. But she preferred to wait outside. "I've been there several times," she told me as I headed inside, "it's too hard." And when I left, all she said was: "It's so, *so*, sad."

The museum, which I mentioned earlier when discussing the question of the uniqueness of conflicts, was established a decade after the genocide and named the Kigali Genocide Memorial. Later the name was extended to include "of the Tutsis," which leaves no room for doubt as to who is guilty and who is the victim. This addition ignores the Hutu victims and the broader context of the long-running fight in which both sides took part. A minimalist and dignified atmosphere, free from any pornographic undertones, prevails within the not-so-large museum. There are few exhibits, but each of them overwhelms the visitor with horror, and the cumulative effect is suffocating. A historical section surveys Rwanda from the precolonial period through the ethnic separation brought about by colonial rule, the suppression of the Tutsi by Hutu rule, the incitement and preparations for the genocide, and the genocide itself. A separate area is dedicated to genocide as a human phenomenon, one that repeated itself throughout the twentieth century, with Rwanda being a particular instance of it. A separate area displays photographs of men, women, and children, each offering the camera the innocent look of someone who can't imagine they will soon become a victim. And then there are videos in which survivors tell what happened to them. Some add to their dry description of the events something of their feelings: their loss of trust in humanity, for example, or a longing so profound that again and again it brings a young man that carries it to spend his days wandering about the mass grave where all the members of his family are buried. Another area displays a small pile – just a tiny sample – of bones, along with several rows of skulls. Another area, unbearably difficult, is dedicated to murdered children. It is also minimalistic, presenting the stories of children along with a single picture of the boy or girl and next to it a name, age (a few weeks old, a few months old, a few years old, an adolescent), a characteristic feature ("loved her mother," "soccer player," "often ill and cried a lot"), and the way in which they were murdered ("skull crushed," "slammed into a wall," "eyes gouged out," "dismemberment of organs"). Outside the building there's a wide, well-maintained garden, breathtaking in its beauty. It takes a few moments to realize – for me it happened under a frangipani tree blooming with bright pink flowers – that this is actually a mass burial site. About 259,000 people (as mentioned before, we only have estimates) are buried under these concrete slabs, each of which is the size of a room. Together they are arranged in such a way as to create a series of long, green boulevards where visitors stroll.

On my second visit to the museum, I was accompanied by J, a man of about seventy years old. He is Tutsi, and perhaps because of this, that is, because he was on the victims' side, he felt less ambivalent and didn't leave my side the entire time. He expanded on the story that the museum tells by adding his own experiences, every few moments pulling a handkerchief out of his pocket and sobbing into it quietly. When the genocide began, he was abroad with his wife and children. Entering the country was impossible, so together with two workers from human rights organizations, he waited at the Burundian border for refugees who were fleeing for their lives. His goal was to assist them and collect testimony about what had happened to them and what was still happening in Rwanda. "I heard over four hundred testimonies," he said while shaking his head from side to side, as if he still had trouble believing that all this really happened. His shoulders, which became more and more slouched as our visit continued, revealed the weight of the stories he carried. The arriving refugees brought news with them of those who were left behind. In this way – while immersed in the horrors of strangers, to whom he provided immediate care for their injuries and physical needs – he learned that his entire family had been murdered. His parents, his seven brothers and sisters, and all their spouses and children. They are all buried in mass graves in the south of the country, where they had lived among their future killers, many of whom J had known since he was a child.

In July, the forces of the Rwandan Patriotic Front (RPF), led by current president Paul Kagame, defeated the governmental forces, first in the capital of Kigali and then in the rest of the country. The RPF seized power and put an end to the killing. Approximately two million Hutus fled for their lives out of fear of revenge. And such acts of revenge indeed took place, some undertaken by Kagame and his men. These Hutus found themselves internally displaced or became refugees in neighboring countries. In addition to the Hutus who were murdered in acts of revenge, many thousands died of disease in overcrowded refugee camps.

Kagame was appointed vice president and minister of defense, and became the most powerful man in an administration overwhelmingly staffed by Tutsi members of the RPF. In 2000, the president resigned, and Kagame was appointed to the position he has held ever since. He has repeatedly been reelected to this position (2003, 2010, 2017 and 2024) without facing any real opponents, in elections that were neither transparent nor free from corruption. In January 2016, following a referendum, the constitution was changed so that Kagame could respond to the "will of the people" and run for a third term as president in August 2017. However, despite his dictatorial rule, Kagame is widely admired in his country and abroad due to the rebuilding process he led, the economic growth he has created, and the reconciliation process he is responsible for – a process that was an explicit goal of his administration.

Rwanda had disintegrated in the most literal sense imaginable. The country's population in April 1994 was seven million. Three months later, in the aftermath of (most of) the bloodshed, the country's population was four million: a million had been murdered and two million had become refugees. The infrastructure was also in tatters: many buildings were uninhabitable, many sheep and cattle had been slaughtered during the massacre, food shortages were acute, clinics and hospitals had been destroyed, roads and dirt roads had been destroyed or were now obstructed by piles of rotting bodies. The stench was terrible, or as B, whom I met on the mountain, in Jali, put it, "dizzying." Senior officials of the defeated Hutu government fled, taking government funds with them and leaving the already impoverished state coffers empty. Many of the wounded – many of them amputees – required immediate medical attention. Orphaned children wandered the streets alone. People – survivors, close relatives of victims, and also those who had taken part in the massacre – were all in a state of shock. One of the first actions the new government had to take – a grotesque act that illustrates the apocalyptic dimensions of the destruction – was to deal with the many stray dogs that had been feeding on the bodies and severed limbs that were scattered everywhere. The sheer quantities, and apparently the blood, turned the dogs into uncontrollable predators. So they were shot and killed.

Kagame took upon himself the task of reconstruction. He was a member of an aristocratic Tutsi family that had been exiled to Uganda in 1959, when the reins of power in Rwanda had begun to pass to the Hutu. Kagame was also the one who led the reconciliation process, our main concern here. However, anyone looking for a resemblance between Kagame and Nelson Mandela (a resemblance that Kagame is keen to create, as can be seen in the promotional video I described earlier) will be disappointed. Mandela, driven by a humanist worldview, fought for equal rights. For him violence was a tactic meant to highlight the problem of discrimination against black people. Violence, he repeated, could never solve a problem. Kagame, by contrast, had been a warrior his entire adult life. First in Uganda, where he was exiled and took part in the coup, then in Rwanda during the civil war. As president he continued to intervene militarily in events in neighboring Congo. For him violence was and remains a tool like any other, a tool to be used when it serves a purpose, even if the purpose is essentially something incompatible with violence. Such as reconciliation.

As vice president and head of security in the government formed immediately after the genocide, Kagame was in charge of the army, which was essentially the RPF under a new name. The army effectively controlled the country, making Kagame the most powerful man in Rwanda even before he was appointed president. He restored order and stopped the bloodshed. Too late, according to his critics, as in the months following the massacre, soldiers (of the Rwandan army, which was actually the RPF) carried out numerous acts of revenge against the Hutu. Once order was restored, Kagame turned to rebuilding the country, a reconstruction that he combined with and even made conditional upon the reconciliation process. The Rwandan reconciliation was thus not born from humanistic or religious values. Later, the church was recruited into the process, and indeed one can find expressions of such values, whether in discourse on human fraternity or in gestures of forgiveness, but the womb that gave birth to this reconciliation was pragmatic, and the midwife – to put it bluntly – was not motivated by love. In what follows, I will address the impact this sad birth has had on reality in Rwanda. The question to be answered here: Is something born from such a birth doomed to be a sad baby, a sad child, and, later on, a sad adult?

Unlike South Africa, where exposing the truth was the foundation upon which the entire process was based, in Rwanda's reconciliation process things were to work differently. Yes, the truth was to be exposed, but in a selective (as opposed to incomplete) manner (more on that later). The truth was seen as important, but it was not the sole, nor the main, element in the process. Punishment was accorded great weight in the concept of justice on which the process was based. It was not enough to tell the truth and accept responsibility; the perpetrators of crimes were required to pay a price for their actions through imprisonment or community service. In some ways, this is a more concrete conception of justice, focusing on (most) actions and (most) people who committed them, and removing from the equation the broad definition of justice (that it should, for example, apply to everyone). It is, moreover, a very tangible, immediate conception of justice, one based on relationships between individuals, one that sees the possibility of repair and reconciliation taking place in the space between them.

According to the Rwandan view, bringing the perpetrators to justice was the path to justice. On a deeper level, traveling this path required addressing the culture of "impunity" that prevailed in this society during the genocide and in the years leading up to it. Such an atmosphere prevailed in the country as a result of the Hutu government and its branches not only taking actions that led to the displacement of Tutsis from positions of power and influence, but also turning a blind eye to cases of Hutu violence against them. The message that no action would be taken against those who harmed Tutsis did what such a message does at any time in any society: it sacrificed the security of the Tutsis at the feet of those Hutus who sought an outlet for their frustration and aggression.

The international community also took its own step. A few months after the genocide, the UN Security Council established the International Criminal Court in Arusha, Tanzania, with the aim of prosecuting the architects of the genocide: the heads of state, heads of security forces, religious leaders, and heads of media outlets behind the incitement. The international community had, in fact, an unusually large presence in the country before the genocide, and therefore had a real ability to stop, or at least try to stop, the bloodshed. There had been 2,500 UN peacekeeping troops stationed in Rwanda since 1993 to implement the Arusha Accords. Warnings of weapons stockpiles and lists of intended victims had reached the UN before the genocide began, but nothing was done. On April 6, 1994, in a disturbing display of selective perception, members of the UN Security Council observed a minute of silence in memory of the Rwandan president whose plane had been shot down, even though the massacre in Rwanda had already begun and the UN troops stationed there were doing nothing to stop it. After Hutu militias murdered ten UN soldiers guarding the prime minister (a Hutu who was perceived to be a moderate and was herself murdered), the UN withdrew most of its forces from the country. Only 250 soldiers stayed behind, and they were instructed not to take any action unless they themselves were in danger. And so the soldiers stood by, and except for a few cases where they allowed Tutsis who had fled for their lives to hide in secured areas, the main thing they did was help foreigners who were in the country at the time to escape this cataclysm. Only in mid-May, more than a month after the genocide began, did the UN determine that "genocidal acts may have been committed" and that a special force should be sent to stop it. Yet this force did not arrive in Rwanda until the end of the massacre, almost two months later.

During the twenty years of the International Criminal Court's work, 3,000 testimonies were heard, 93 indictments were filed, 75 trials were held, and 61 people were convicted. The court was also the first international body to recognize rape, previously seen as one of the unpleasant side effects of war, as a war crime in its own right. It should be noted that the International Criminal Court did not address the civil war that culminated in the genocide, nor the criminal acts of vengeance committed by RPF fighters, that is, the crimes of the victorious side – the side that dictated the narrative according to which the Tutsi alone were the victims and the Hutu alone the victimizers. In this sense, the UN supported the narrative of the Kagame administration. This approach even led to the dismissal of the chief prosecutor, Carla Del Ponte, after she announced that she had gathered enough evidence to justify an investigation into crimes committed by RPF fighters during the genocide.

Despite all this, the Rwandan government, led by Kagame, expressed hostility toward the International Criminal Court, which sought to prosecute the architects of the genocide but not its perpetrators. Kagame and his government were suspicious of the motives of the countries that led the effort to establish the court, particularly those of the West. After all, these countries stood by while the genocide was taking place and so had a clear interest in clearing their consciences. "The International Court is a fraud reminiscent of imperialism and colonialism," Kagame said.

The Rwandan government therefore took it upon itself to prosecute *all* those who took part in the genocide. However, in doing so, it encountered technical difficulties, mainly due to the huge number of defendants and a legal system that, after the genocide, had only a handful of judges and lawyers left. In 2000, between 120,000 and 130,000 detainees were crowded into prisons with a combined capacity of 12,000 to 15,000. A minority of them were brought to justice, the rest were left waiting. Other suspects were not yet arrested, so they roamed freely among their victims. According to the concept of justice that guided the reconstruction process, it was impossible to move toward reconciliation without going through the process of prosecution and punishment. But if the authorities had continued to prosecute suspects using the traditional Western legal system, as they had done in the years since the genocide, it would have taken over a century to address all the cases. In other words, the reconstruction process was paralyzed, and so was the larger society, which was in a kind of hell, both in the concrete sense of its still-bleeding wounds and in the existential sense of being in limbo. The genocide was over, but the country was still not on the path to recovery.

The government turned to *gacaca*, which, as mentioned earlier, is an ancient local tradition designed to resolve conflicts within the community and a routine part of life in Rwanda.

When a conflict arose between members of the community, its members gathered on the grass (hence the name: gacaca is "grass" in Kinyarwanda), listened to the parties – and, if necessary, witnesses – and made a decision or proposed a solution. This conflict resolution mechanism was modified according to the demands of the moment; namely, the prosecution of many people. The choice of gacaca also reflected an understanding that a way had to be found to enable victims and aggressors to live together. This mechanism, emphasizing the connective tissue of the community, brought victims and aggressors together and was in effect the first, at times unbearable, step in the process of reconciliation. "The hardest thing," J explained to me after we left the memorial museum together, "is to look each other in the eye, because the natural reaction of victims and perpetrators is to reject or avoid each other. That's why I call it a painstaking exercise." It's worth considering the etymology of that word, painstaking – taking pains. This exercise required pain. The fact that the explicit and declared aim of bringing criminals to justice was to enable the victims to forgive them, to welcome them back into society, and to build a life together set the tone for the entire process. The victims and the aggressors were actors in a play whose final act is well known: reconciliation.

The gacacas were a hybrid of sorts: part amateur courts, part truth and reconciliation commissions. Each community elected their own representatives, who underwent a brief training and became judges. They wore a ribbon in the colors of the Rwandan flag with the words *gacaca* and *inyangamugayo* – "those who hate dishonesty" in Kinyarwanda. There were cases in which it was discovered, during the hearings, that some of those elected as judges had participated in the massacres. They were suspended from their positions and transferred to the side of the accused. All this says something about the complexity of the situation and the larger social fabric, and about the lack of professionalism in the system, which, among other things, had neither prosecutors nor defense attorneys.

Community members gathered in their public places – on the ground or grass, sometimes under a tree. The judges sat on chairs, sometimes with a table, notebooks, and writing utensils, sometimes without. There were no stands, no stages, and not even defined – or separate – areas where the victims, witnesses, and accused (including those still living in the community and those brought from prison for the hearings) sat. Everyone sat together – old, young, children, and infants – listening to confessions, requests for forgiveness, and pardons. Whoever was speaking simply stood up, surrounded by the community members, who sat together and formed a human cluster of pain. When someone finished speaking, he or she sat back down to join the group. The others listened in silence. Sometimes victims would break down in tears while listening to the recounting of an event that occurred during the genocide. The rest would wait in silence, and once they calmed down or were taken aside by members of the community, whose bodies concealed them while they wept, the proceedings continued.

Emphasis was placed on the healing power of revealing the truth for victims and its liberating power for criminals. The prison sentences of those who confessed to their crimes were shortened or commuted to community service, often in the very same community in which they had committed their crimes. Thus there was a direct and visible connection between the act and the punishment, between destruction and repair. Those who committed crimes were asked not only *what* they did and *how* they did it, but also *why* they did it and whether they did it *voluntarily* or because they were threatened. This question regarding degrees of freedom is significant not only in relation to the aggressors and the extent to which they could choose whether to take part in the genocide. It affected the entire reconciliation process. The gacaca trials touched on the question of free choice for all citizens of the country, victims and victimizers alike, because the decision to use this prosecution mechanism was taken by those in power. Then, as is customary in Rwanda, it was imposed on the people and carried out as instructed. Gacaca trials were held in every community in the country. There were over 12,000 such courts, and participation in them was not optional. Anyone who refused to take part in them was liable to a prison sentence of one to six months.

In the decade during which this mechanism operated, almost two million cases were tried and 1.3 million people were prosecuted. That is, at a scale unprecedented anywhere in the world. This process made it possible to bring criminals to justice (though their sentences were reduced if they confessed), to reveal the fate of many who were killed, and to locate makeshift graves (mostly mass graves) in order to bring the dead to a proper burial (mostly mass graves too, since so much time had passed and it was difficult to identify the bodies or their parts). However, much of the truth was not revealed. Many victims, especially women who were raped, chose not to speak about what had happened to them out of shame, as they continued to live in their communities. And crimes committed by the RPF, that is, Tutsis, which threatened to undermine the narrative of Tutsis-as-victims and Hutus-as-victimizers, were silenced. At the end of the gacaca trials, 37,000 people remained in prison. The rest had been returned to their communities.

This was precisely the practical need that reconciliation came to address: Tutsis and Hutus live together in this country and a way had to be found to allow them to continue doing so. The gacaca provided an answer both to the (relatively) formal task of bringing criminals to justice and to the desire to reveal the truth of (most) victims. And the government also took steps that were intended to provide a response to the softer aspect of living together – a shared narrative. Before the civil war and genocide people spoke in terms of Tutsi and Hutu. The new narrative spoke of one country where everyone was Rwandan. Ethnic registration on identity cards was abolished and it was now forbidden to even talk about which ethnic group a person belonged to. Another layer in the new narrative was, as mentioned, the rigid (and sometimes false) dichotomy between victim (Tutsi) and aggressor (Hutu). Although, in order to make this narrative more palatable, an explanation was added regarding all the many Hutus who took part in the genocide: they had been brainwashed by the extremist Hutu government.

The reconciliation process did not end there. Moving past the domain of narrative, reconciliation was translated into daily life in an immediate and tangible way, and the population was not given time to get used to it incrementally. In effect, reconciliation was applied to all of the country's social structures: schools, workplaces, and churches. Hutus and Tutsis share all of these places, and thus all these social structures were mobilized for the realization of a shared life. Similarly, efforts to rebuild and later develop the country were also folded into the institutional reconciliation effort: every project had to (and still must) prove that all members of the community, Hutu and Tutsi, are partners in it. And preference is given to those who were immediate victims or victimizers: the widow of a victim and the wife of the man who murdered him, for example.

V is a stormy, theatrical woman (according to the restrained norms of Rwandan society) in her fifties, and a Tutsi. She speaks quietly, but incessantly and melodiously, the sound somewhat reminiscent of a murmured prayer. As she talks, she peppers her addressee with soft, but purposeful, touches. The effect is a kind of subtle yet firm assurance that there's no escaping her. I spent three days with her, when she participated in a training that we gave at a community health and nutrition center. Although she wanted to set up a partnership between us and her small organization – one she founded after returning with her family from exile in the Congo immediately after the genocide – she had difficulty concentrating on the training. From the moment she and I agreed that at the end of the day we would sit together and talk privately (a tête-à-tête, she suggested, her voice indulgent and eager), her need to share became so urgent that she could not restrain herself.

She followed me around, grabbing my arm to pull me closer even as I ran the training. Every time our conversation was interrupted, she would remember exactly where we left off and would continue from that point at the first possible opportunity, an opportunity she often manufactured.

"Who in your case, in the Holy Land, is the 'Tutsi' and who is the 'Hutu'?" she whispered in my ear. This was her way of asking who the good guys and the bad guys are in our conflict, since in her eyes the Hutus were the absolute bad and the Tutsis were the absolute good. Unlike other Tutsis I spoke to, I detected no empathy in her for the Hutus who were also victims, nor any willingness to see the genocide in the context of a larger conflict in which there were two sides.

"I think with us, each side sees itself as the victim," I replied.

"Aaaah," she slurred, and then capped this off with a short, terse statement: "*That* is not good."

Despite her emotions, V plays an active, indeed daily, role in one of the tangible expressions of Rwandan reconciliation. The organization she heads is designed to support women at risk, that is, women who were left alone after the genocide, either because their partner was murdered or because he is in prison. The women her organization supports come together in small agricultural cooperatives, usually in pairs, but under this particular condition: in order to receive support (from the state to the organization and from the organization to the women) each pair must include someone from the victim's side and someone from the side of the victimizers. "You see," she said, holding my arm and stroking my back, "sometimes both women have been infected with AIDS by the same man, who was the husband of one of them and the rapist of the other. Sometimes the husband of one is in prison for murdering the husband of the other. We even have a cooperative of two women in which the husband of one murdered the baby of the other. He did it right in front of her eyes. The baby was ten months old, and this man – who is in prison but will soon be released because he confessed to his actions and accepted responsibility for them, so his sentence has been shortened – slammed the baby's head against a wall and crushed it." She continued looking at me with a grave expression, as if expecting something I couldn't quite put my finger on. After a long moment, she asked, "What do you say about that?"

I responded with the only thing I could say at that moment: "I don't know what to say."

V nodded. The intensity of her gaze subsided, along with the urgency that had accompanied our communication all that day. Perhaps my speechlessness was the effect she was looking for. Perhaps she saw in it a sign that I recognized the inconceivable difficulty of a life with an outer layer of reconciliation and an inner core of pain.

As was the case with the gacaca, the government was able to harness other ancient Rwandan traditions that strengthened the new national identity and fostered a national pride corrupted by the genocide. An example of this is Umuganda, a tradition that literally means "joining together for a common purpose." Traditionally this found its expression in mutual aid: a person faced with a difficult task would ask his family, friends, and neighbors for help, and they would all work together to do what the task required. In precolonial, colonial, and independent Rwanda, the authorities used this tradition to mobilize the population for public works. During the days of the massacre, there were those in local government who took advantage of this custom and its tradition of obedience in order to fuel the killing machine. In other words: they ensured that the instructions to kill, which came from above, were duly carried out by the masses. In post-genocide Rwanda, the tradition of Umuganda has been reorganized and incorporated into daily life, thus becoming a means for rebuilding state and society, and for realizing the reconciliation that this rebuilding demands. Every last Saturday of the month, the country comes to a standstill: no work, no school, no religious services, and no commerce. The only driving permitted is that which helps realize a communal goal. All citizens aged eighteen to sixty-five are required to take part in works for the benefit of the community: construction, gardening, digging drainage ditches, painting road margins or buildings, and cleaning. (This obsessive cleaning is another sign of the unnatural feeling one can sense throughout the country. This cleanliness is at odds with a normal, free life, one in which places get dirty from time to time.) Children hang around the workers and help as well, and those who cannot take part in the work due to illness or old age sit next to the workers and do their part by offering advice. Armed soldiers and police make sure that everyone participates in this very tangible expression of reconciliation: former enemies are partners in building a common future.

Commemoration plays an important role in the reconciliation process and is seen as both a moral obligation toward the victims and a means for education. Memorial sites for the victims of the massacre have been established all over the country, even in the smallest villages. Sometimes churches serve as memorial sites, sometimes a room in a public building – a clinic or a school. Sometimes there's a monument, sometimes a mass grave. Usually the memorial site is erected at the place where the massacre took place – in a particular church, particular room, particular clinic – and a sign details how many Tutsis were murdered there. Often this figure is only an approximation, because some bodies weren't found or body parts that were found couldn't be matched to a particular victim. Some sites also display human remains from a massacre, shelves with skulls arranged in rows, for example.

Genocide is a presence that cannot be escaped. Even places where there is no monument or other marker carry the memory of the massacre. I often felt there that I was in a society where I was the only one who didn't see or hear the specific ghosts of the specific individuals who were murdered, who continue to roam among the living, looking at them with piercing eyes of incrimination, longing, and shock.

On the shores of Lake Kivu, at the western border of Rwanda, I sat in a small café that served delicious Rwandan coffee – a rarity, as the local coffee, known for its quality, is mostly intended for export, so a cup of coffee like this is hard to come by. The view was breathtaking and the sunset added all that a sunset can add. For a moment I was able to forget about everything, even the terrible, inescapable poverty, whose consequences are evident even in more affluent parts of the country.

"So beautiful," I shared my feelings with M, a driver who accompanied us on those days we left the city. M had never met Israelis, and when we first met, he frowned as if trying to remember something or organize his thoughts. Then he said: "Israel . . . eh— (a long, melodious sound that indicates a kind of 'yes'). Jerusalem, right? You are the Jews and Arabs who are always at war?"

He nodded quietly while also looking at the lake and the sky, then said, laconically and without looking back at me: "This water is *full* of people. Some threw the bodies there after they were murdered and some drowned alive. They tied them up and threw them into the water."

Every year, the hundred days between April and July are dedicated to the commemoration of the hundred days of the genocide. Most of the events are concentrated in April, when all the institutions in the country take part in the commemorative activities. Like many other things in Rwanda, remembrance is a national enterprise. I spoke about memory and commemoration with G, a science teacher in his late twenties, whose shy brown eyes literally sparkled when he spoke about education and science. When I met him again a year later, he was already serving in a senior position as a member of President Kagame's advisory committee on technology and science education. His eyes sparkled less and his speech had grown more cautious, but it was important for him to convey to me – with glances and subtle references to our conversation from the year before – that he remained the same man, that he had perhaps matured a little, but not for the worse.

He was eight years old at the time of the genocide, and among the lucky ones who managed to escape. He and his family were exiled to Congo, where they lived in a refugee camp for three years.

"There was nothing," he told me about those days as we walked together along a dirt path winding between the huts that serve as classrooms at the boarding school. "Nothing, certainly no schools, so we didn't study."

Since then, it seems, he has constantly been making up for all that he missed. Like a thirsty man who cannot be quenched, he studies with an astonishing passion for learning and tries to instill it in the children he teaches. The classroom walls, for example, have been covered with faded, homemade prints of Leonardo da Vinci's drawings of machines and inventions. "That way it gets into them without them even realizing it," he explained with pleasure.

"And the forgiveness, is it real?" I asked, cautiously, aware that I was approaching the realm of the "three dots" that mark what cannot be spoken about. Yet I could not let go of this question that, it seemed to me, goes to the heart of the very possibility of reconciliation.

G suddenly stopped.

I stopped too and stood beside him, silent.

He looked down at the dirt path, as if there was something meaningful there for him to find.

It was clear that I had gone beyond what one was allowed to ask, so I let it go. We started walking again along the dirt path, talking about education and science, when suddenly he interrupted me – an unusual act according to Rwandan etiquette – and said quietly: "It's just . . . it's not acceptable," he said in an apologetic tone.

I signaled my understanding with a small nod and an embarrassed smile, which was mainly intended to relieve his embarrassment at the unacceptable step he had taken when he interrupted me and put me in my place. We continued walking and discussing other topics. A few moments later, when we were far enough out of earshot of others, he picked up the thread of our conversation that he had dropped only moments before.

"Yes, it's real," he answered my direct question and then expanded, as if in response to the one I didn't ask: "You know, not everything needs to be understood. I don't completely understand it either, so I tell myself that maybe only someone who's gone through it can truly understand."

I felt the corners of my lips curling slightly upward with embarrassment. My arrogant insistence, perhaps typical of someone from the Global North, to comprehend everything had been exposed. He continued: "You see a woman whose entire family was murdered, and she listens to the murderer talk about it – he literally describes how he did it – and at the end she stands up and hugs him and tells him she forgives him. No," his head shook resolutely from side to side as if he were reexamining things and reaching the same conclusion again, "There are things I don't understand so I tell myself that maybe it's a matter of deciding – you decide to forgive, and you forgive."

G continued to speak with growing intensity, as if an urgent need to get me to understand had emerged in him during our conversation. He drew attention to what we had in common, as two people who were observing something we could discuss, and also discussing the fact that we were discussing something that neither of us fully understood. But then he helped me see the leap I needed to make if I were to cross this abyss of not understanding. He held my hand, figuratively, so that I could jump with him. "And here's another thing I can't understand," he added, returning to the matter of understanding before expanding on his answer, "You see a doctor who has been a doctor his whole life and that's what he knows how to do, right? Heal people. Then one day he receives an order and takes a machete in his hands and murders the people he's been taking care of up until that day. I ask myself: Is this even a human being?"

"And what do you tell yourself?" I asked what I thought he wanted me to ask.

"No," he concluded, "that's not a human being, it's a monster. And it's very important to understand this, so that's why we have this month of remembrance, to hear these stories and then be by ourselves and contemplate it all."

"And has anything changed for you with the perspective of twenty years of being by yourself and contemplating these things?"

For a few moments he nodded silently, his arms crossed. "Yes." He looked at me with his eyes sparkling. "I think so. I think the most important thing I've discovered through this process is that this monster exists in all of us. You and me both, if they brainwashed us like they did those murderers, the monster might come out of us and erase the fact that we are human. That's what these days of remembrance give me, to know that it's in all of us and to know what to be careful of. And it's also for remembering. I think that if I were murdered, I would want to be remembered."

I told him about the research being conducted by one of the two white people I met in Rwanda, a French psychologist who was there to do research for her thesis on the trauma of genocide victims. The question she chose to investigate was whether or not the memorial events held between April and July help the victims. In a quintessential display of science revealing the obvious, she found that the memorial events exacerbated symptoms of depression and anxiety among the victims.

G listened patiently, then smiled at me with forgiveness and replied with the closest thing to irony I would encounter in Rwanda: "But this is not a psychological question; this is an educational question."

G's statement could be an interesting starting point for examining the reconciliation process. It reflects that which is emphasized in Rwandan society, a society that acknowledges individual suffering, but does not sanctify it and doesn't place it as a spoke in the wheel of the collective good. If the collective good is a shared life, and shared life requires reconciliation, and reconciliation must pass through all sorts of stations, memory, for example, then the individual must accept that his difficulty in dealing with the pain of the past is second in importance to the collective's project of commemoration. Therefore the choice of whether to deal with it, when, and in what manner is not his to make; this belongs to the collective. In much the same way, forgiveness is seen as a gift that victims give to society so that it can be reconciled, and Hutus accept their silence as the price they must pay – a kind of collective punishment – for the complete moral failure of their "group." In fact, this is the guiding principle of the entire process: the common good is defined as reconciliation, and everything else derives from this: justice, truth, repair, and most certainly free choice. And just as reconciliation was born, as a constraint that emerged to meet a practical need, naked of higher values, so also all that derives from it is somewhat naked and perhaps even forced.

The concept of justice underpinning this reconciliation process was based on uncovering the truth and doling out punishment. Indeed, a large number of victims spoke about what they had gone through and were recognized, while a large number of the genocide's perpetrators were brought to justice. However, it seems reasonable to me to claim that the justice that was done was selective, because it was the justice of the victors, formulated and implemented by them. Unlike the victors in South Africa, who were able to create a narrative that even most on the losing side could live with, here the losing side has been neglected. They were, to put it simply, sent to stand in the corner. Unlike South Africa, where justice at the individual level was sacrificed for justice at the collective level, here individual and collective justice on one side was sacrificed for justice on the other – and it's debatable whether such a version still meets the definition of justice. This means, at the most basic level, that the voices of Hutus who were also victims are almost never heard. And the stories of Hutus who acted heroically, risking their lives to save Tutsis, are present in the new Rwandan narrative but are not emphasized nearly enough.

This is quite unlike their South African counterparts: white people who opposed apartheid have been given special weight. It is also, in many ways, unlike the equivalent Jewish-Israeli narrative, which glorifies righteous gentiles.

Such selective justice has practical implications as well. Most aid programs – scholarships and mental health care, for example – are intended for victims who belong to the victors' side. This is a remarkable stretch of the concept of justice, sometimes absurdly so. K, a social worker at an orphanage in Kigali, for example, is the son of a Tutsi father and a Hutu mother. His father, who worked for the Red Cross and was murdered on the first day of the genocide, foresaw the future and sent K, who was then a child, to Kenya with his uncle. K returned to Rwanda after the genocide and grew up with his mother, who, because she is Hutu, is not recognized as a victim and is not entitled to the assistance she would have been entitled to (including assistance for her son) if she had been a Tutsi widow.

Similar to the South African reconciliation process, in Rwanda emphasis was placed on uncovering the truth. However, in South Africa justice and truth were almost synonymous, whereas here the element of punishment was added, which was of great importance and was perceived as a necessity without which reconciliation would not be possible. Another, more significant difference is that in South Africa a truth was revealed whose existence could not be denied, except (perhaps, and at times) the degree of responsibility of this or that person in relation to it. By contrast, in Rwanda a great and painful truth was revealed, but only that truth which concerns the victims of one side, the victorious one. To be sure, this is a strong and powerful truth. But like justice – whose realization may be incomplete, though it's doubtful that it can have dead zones – the question arises whether selective truth (as opposed, of course, to relative truth) is still truth at all.

The question of repair received an interesting answer in the Rwandan reconciliation process. It was very different from the South African answer, partly because most of the crimes were committed by people who knew their victims, and relatively close in time to the beginning of the process. The connection between the crime and its object was direct and immediate, as was the redress: the one who committed the crime paid with imprisonment or community service, the fate of the one who was murdered was revealed, and his body was brought for burial. A destroyed house was rebuilt, a field that had been destroyed was reworked, a refugee (Tutsi or Hutu) was returned to his community. In other words, someone who committed a crime could ask for forgiveness from the specific person against whom the crime was committed. Someone who had a crime committed against him could forgive the specific person who asked for forgiveness. What was destroyed could be rebuilt. On the surface, this seemingly simple connection between the crime and the redress ignores the difference in their particular weight. It is hard to accept that asking for forgiveness somehow balances out the crimes committed, just as it was difficult for many Israelis to accept that the German government's reparations could be weighed against the crimes committed in the Holocaust. To be sure, the crimes and the redress are not comparable. Yet it seems to me that over the years a certain understanding of all this has taken hold. If, after all, it is impossible for anything to be comparable to such crimes, this arrangement is nothing more than an act of signaling. The perpetrator signals acceptance of responsibility and the victim signals their willingness to acknowledge this acceptance of responsibility.

The question of free choice in the Rwandan reconciliation process raises great difficulties, and perhaps this needs to be said explicitly: there was very little freedom of choice involved. The entire population was required to take part in the gacaca hearings. The rehabilitation programs dictate cooperation between former enemies. And by being forced to live together, large parts of Rwandan society continue to experience a kind of violence, as they must live alongside – and thus see on a very regular basis – those who committed crimes against them and their families. The possibility of changing their place of residence in order to move away from a living memory is only theoretical for most. This is a poor population, and overwhelmingly agricultural, so people's livelihoods and very existence are fundamentally tied to their land. Even today, more than three decades after the genocide, people tilling their land may suddenly discover human bones – of their relatives, of their neighbors, and sometimes of those they themselves murdered. So when it comes to the freedom of choice at the heart of the Rwandan reconciliation process, the situation can be summed up roughly like this: We are reconciling. Period.

And so a significant question is posed: Is the Rwandan reconciliation process, despite all this, worth it? I feel that raising this question here obliges me to try to convey something of the raw feeling that one gets when visiting Rwanda and when trying to explore this issue. It is a kind of moral obligation that I owe to the people I spoke to, all of whom – without exception, both Hutu and Tutsi, including those who were critical of the reconciliation process – told me: "But first, go to the memorial museum." So maybe that is where we should start: every foreigner must go to the genocide memorial museum. Such a requirement isn't written anywhere, but neither is saying "hello" or "thank you," yet it's widely seen as normal behavior that exists thanks to society's unwritten codes. Like everything else in Rwanda, the entire society is mobilized for this commemoration. In Israel every official visitor at every political level is taken to visit Yad Vashem. In Rwanda it's hard to meet a regular person who doesn't ask: "And have you been to the museum?" This is a heartbreaking question, as it implies the statement: Before you look at us, before you criticize our reconciliation process, you must understand what we have been through. And perhaps this is the ultimate point: you cannot address their reconciliation process without understanding where they were three decades ago, without seeing the dust and ashes from which they have risen.

It is therefore perhaps proper to return to the definition of reconciliation that Rwandan society has set for itself: living together. In this sense, their success is difficult to challenge: there has been no ethnic bloodshed for over three decades.

Perhaps a heroic, romantic reconciliation, reconciliation as we imagine it, is simply not possible for a generation that experienced this conflict and in many ways is still steeped in its ugliness. This generation of Rwandans, who have many characteristics of those who humbly accept punishment for something they deserve, bow their heads for the sake of the next generation. Like the South African reconciliation, the Rwandan reconciliation must be placed on a timeline. In the reconciling present, the justice being done is selective, sometimes twisted. But into their reconciled future a generation is growing up that is not accustomed to divisive ethnic discourse; equality between a Hutu child and a Tutsi child is anchored both in the law and in the nation's new narrative. Perhaps the best illustration of the possibility of a common future is embodied in the fact that marriages between Hutu and Tutsi – even between the children of those who were victims and those who were victimizers – are seen as something positive and desirable, proof that the next generation is no longer sick with the disease of ethnic segregation.

There are those who see the reconciliation that has been achieved as a temporary and volatile situation imposed by a dictatorial regime. Ethnic awareness exists and simmers beneath the surface, even if it is not spoken about. With this comes the knowledge that their process of doing justice left large areas unaddressed. But one can argue the opposite: even given this awareness and these currents, the memory of the genocide is alive and pulsing, to the point that it has become a force that drives and sustains this ongoing reconciliation process. Yes, it contains artificial, impossible, repressed, and unfair elements, but it is peaceful, it is free from violence, and it brings with it the possibility of a better future and a new generation of Rwandans in no way accustomed to ethnic distinctions.

So what will be?

Only time will tell.

5

Layers

MY EXPLORATION OF RECONCILIATION in South Africa and Rwanda was and remains an active, intentional exploration by someone searching for clues to that elusive thing we are dealing with here: reconciliation. Although the cases I have described differ from each other in almost every conceivable way – historical circumstances, power relations, international involvement, leaders, and the nature of the reconciliation process itself – there are similarities between these reconciling societies, elements that may illuminate the bare minimum that is necessary for reconciliation. My journey in search of this missing element involved a kind of peeling away: I removed layer after layer of the characteristics I found in these reconciling societies and examined each one with an eye on a single criterion: necessity.

Among the layers I peeled away, I found noble and inspiring elements, some of the finer expressions of humanity, and yet I discovered that most of them were not essential to the existence of reconciliation, at least not in its early stages. This was, to be honest, something of a disappointment. I was perhaps even a little insulted, since many of these elements are fundamental to my worldview and the closest thing I have to a faith. When I draw near to a believer, when I want to understand him and put myself in his shoes, I remind myself of the deep conviction I have in these elements of humanism. I challenge myself with the question of how much I am able and willing to move away from them. My difficulty in doing so brings me somewhat closer to what in other senses remains a mystery to me.

But I put aside all those lovely, unnecessary layers because what I was looking for was the heart – even though all the while I didn't know whether there was one. That is, I wasn't sure if reconciliation was an onion or an artichoke. Günter Grass likens peeling an onion to the process of remembering, an image that has troubled me since the day I read his autobiography. His metaphor implies a pessimistic view of human consciousness, or at least of our ability to understand anything about it. The idea that beneath layer upon layer of memory there lies no particular cause, factor, or event, and, in other words, that beneath layer upon layer there is nothing – at least nothing we can perceive – does not sit well with my logic. I will admit to finding beauty in an additional implication of his image, which is that human consciousness is too complex to be reduced to a single, foundational cause, factor, or event. But here the reduction I'm seeking is not related to human consciousness, nor to one of its more elusive parts – memory. I'm interested in a personal and social process whose building blocks, unlike consciousness, are visible and observable. And what I'm trying to do is understand them.

So I'll put it simply: Reconciliation is an artichoke. Unlike an onion, which is nothing but layers and which has no heart distinct from them, when you peel away at reconciliation you get to the heart. Still, it is difficult for me to give up these layers, which are important but not necessary. Not only because they're the building blocks of my worldview, but because, given a climate of reconciliation and that variable that can make what first seemed oxymoronic logical – namely, time, these layers can develop and become an integral part of reconciliation, which, as mentioned, is something that is continually emerging, even in a society that has already passed beyond the threshold of conflict.

So allow me just one more moment. Before I get to the heart of the matter, I want to linger a little bit longer on some of those characteristics and note them, however briefly, so that we have something to aspire to.

A Layer That Knows No Boundaries: Empathy

One of the most difficult characteristics of a society in conflict is its patterns of consciousness, patterns that close off one's access to empathy. Empathy, by its very nature, seeks to touch everything. These barriers to empathy result from the survival reflex of a structure trying to preserve itself. After all, if empathy succeeds in breaking through the patterns of a consciousness in conflict, they will dissolve. However, empathy cannot be fenced off in one area without being reduced elsewhere. This can be seen by noting the internal fragmentation that exists within each party to a conflict. This fragmentation and its side effects – the collapse of comradeship and solidarity – worsen as the conflict intensifies and continues, and as the sense of helplessness in relation to the conflict spreads. Israelis know this all too well.

Yet empathy is perhaps the most important foundation of human relationships. It is at the root of our ability to love, forgive, understand, stand in solidarity, and show generosity. Empathy is not dependent on the recipient, in the sense that a person does not have to be worthy of one's empathy to be given it. Empathy doesn't need an external reason; it is in itself the reason, something one practices so that there will be more of it in the world. At the deepest level, at the level that challenges most of us (that is, not at the level of our relationships with loved ones, friends, or members of our "group"), empathy is expressed in one's ability to see the individual apart from the "group" to which he belongs. At the same time, empathy asks that we see this person within the context of his subjective perception of himself and his life. This means seeing him as he sees himself, not through the patterns of one's own conflict-produced consciousness, which reduces and flattens him.

I encountered such empathy in an orphanage near Kigali with G, the young science teacher I mentioned earlier. "This monster is in all of us," he told me, referring to the "ordinary" Hutus who took part in the genocide committed against his tribe. "Both you and I, if we were brainwashed like the murderers, the monster might come out of us and erase the fact that we are human."

And I encountered such empathy with T, in one of the poor agricultural areas outside Cape Town, in a school where children from kindergarten to twelfth grade study. They all wear the same uniform – a short- or long-sleeve white button-down shirt, a dark blue sweater or cardigan with a V-neck, gray pants or a skirt – but these are distinguished by varying degrees of dirt and wear. Some of the many feet jauntily running around are in shoes or sandals, but some are barefoot. And there are children whose bellies are swollen from malnutrition. T, the school's principal, and a dandy of sorts, is stern and humorless. He wanted to be a researcher in medicine, but his parents pushed him toward education because, being colored (a definition that, as mentioned, took root during the apartheid era to denote those of mixed ethnic background and remains common and accepted even in the new South Africa), his chances of getting accepted to study medicine or science, not to mention find work afterward, were slim at best. His high school and university years were tumultuous and lasted much longer than his studies should have required. He participated in demonstrations and strikes against apartheid, and there were long periods when the institutions where he studied were shut down. He was a member of the ANC student organization and later its teachers' organization. Today, however, he is quite critical of the direction the organization has taken since it came to power, especially in recent years. T was one of the more bitter people I met in South Africa. He grieves the life he's wasted, a waste he blames on apartheid. He constantly looks back at the past and what he missed out on because of circumstances – the education he didn't get, the career he might have had. Even today, when he looks at South Africa, he is not satisfied.

"The whites still have most of the resources and most of the opportunities," he explained, "and it will take us many more years to fix what apartheid ruined. But," he continued, "this attitude of 'we'll take what we deserve now and don't care about anything else' is not me," he said, referring to the conduct of the ANC-led regime.

Our conversation was long and meandering, its many branches leading to stories of what apartheid cost his family members and friends. All the while I sensed that the conversation was driven by some urgency he felt to make me understand how evil apartheid was, even though at the same time there was a heartbreaking resignation in his inability to do so. Another school bell reminded me again of our troubled existence, as these bells, like those in other schools I visited in South Africa, sound exactly like the sirens in Israel. Each time I heard one I found myself cringing and momentarily forgetting that I was in what seemed like a parallel universe to the one I left at home.

We shook hands and said goodbye. But when I was already at the threshold of his office door, my back to him, he called out to me, "Maya? Wait a minute."

I turned to him. His eyes were sad but expectant, like a spaceship sending a probe off into the unknown. For a moment I preferred the victim-like, bitter version of him to the one that now appeared before me: full of pain, more mature, recognizing the intricacies of human existence, understanding that what is done cannot truly be undone, and seeking to teach me a thing or two about what he learned firsthand – how infinitely complex it all is.

"There's something you have to understand," he said. "The thing is, *white* people were victims of apartheid too. Apartheid eroded *their* humanity too."

A former victim who can see the victimhood of his former victimizers is a sign of a society that is in the process of reconciliation. But such stunning expressions of empathy can also be heard in our own neck of the woods, so what's actually the difference between here and there?

Well, there is a difference, and it lies in the context, that is, in the attitude of a society toward such expressions. In a society steeped in conflict, such an expression is perceived as a threat (rightly so, from the perspective of the conflict). In a reconciling society, by contrast, such an expression is perceived as heroism, sometimes as a rare and esoteric heroism, true, but certainly not as something worthy of condemnation.

Empathy, or more precisely its absence, has another side, one that is both painful and relevant for those of us in Israel. We tend to take pride in those manifestations of brotherhood and solidarity that still remain in Israeli society, whether they are expressed in mutual aid or in relation to human life, as can be found in cases of captive soldiers, for example, and, more recently, citizens held hostage. At the same time, we tend to look down on those on the other side of the conflict, because in our view they are not "blessed" with these qualities, since their attitude toward human life is "different."

O is an energetic, not to mention restless, autodidact full of humor and charm. In the past, he was, among other things, a teacher, and today he works with learning technologies out of the belief that education is the only cure for the ills of apartheid that are still present among the nonwhite population of South Africa. In his youth, he was saved from what he calls certain death thanks to his father, who one evening during the riots of the 1980s invited him to an after-dinner coffee on the open doorstep of their home. O excitedly told me how his father then said to him: "Shh . . . Listen, do you hear? Listen to the sounds of gunfire. In the morning we'll wake up and count the bodies of young, promising black men like you, who fought the security forces in a just struggle. But they'll no longer be of any use to the struggle, because they'll be dead. Do you want to help South Africa? Stay alive. You're of no use as a corpse."

However, when O talks about empathy, he talks about its other side, which is sad and infuriating. It exemplifies how much empathic ability is a result of a person's and a society's self-perception, and that as these erode, so erodes empathy. This side is also sad and infuriating because it demonstrates how much a lack of empathy can blind people from seeing the damage they are responsible for in someone on the other side of the conflict. This lack blinds them, to the point that they attribute such damage to the victim's supposedly inferior character traits and thus justify the continued injustice they inflict on him.

The greatest damage apartheid caused in the nonwhite population, according to O, was the decay of empathy. "During the apartheid years, it was very much eroded," he explained angrily. "And even today it's not what I would like to see, and it's not what I see in other places, both in Africa and beyond. And I'll explain to you why I think that's the case," he said excitedly, his teaching past still evident in the didactic tone with which he speaks about everything. "It's because when you oppress someone, what you're essentially telling them is: You're *worth*less. There's nothing of value in *you*. And when people live like this, it penetrates into them, it penetrates deeply into their self-perception, even if in their minds they know that they're living in an oppressive situation. And someone who feels that they are less, that there is nothing of value in *them*, cannot conceive that there is something they can *give* to others. And so the oppressor eliminates empathy in the society he oppresses and then uses this to justify the oppression, because he tells himself that it is impossible to treat equally someone who cannot even show empathy to his brothers and sisters, someone who is thus at war with himself."

Of all my many conversations with the humorous T, who insists on focusing on the positive and the possible, the one that touched on the erosion of empathy among the victims of apartheid was the one that got him most worked up, the one that made the arteries on his neck swell with rage.

A Layer That Is Only Pain: Forgiveness

In South Africa, as in Rwanda, all my conversations about reconciliation passed through the subject of forgiveness. Some spoke of forgiveness as a religious imperative. Some see it as an informed decision arising from a practical need. Some elevate it to the level of a sacrifice that a person makes for the benefit of the collective within which he lives, a kind of social duty or gentlemanly gesture. And there are those whose positions are conflicted.

Wherever reconciliation is discussed, forgiveness is discussed as well. And for good reason. Forgiveness has enormous healing power, for both the forgiver and the forgiven. The forgiver powerfully rediscovers himself through an act that redefines him in relation to the one who hurt him, that is, the one who first took away something of his power. The act of forgiveness allows the forgiven to leave the corner into which he had retreated or been sent in shame. Forgiveness frees the parties from the sick, painful relationship that binds them close together. It allows them to redefine this relationship, because this is what reconciliation is: a redefinition of relationships.

And yet here I am writing about forgiveness as one of the layers of reconciliation rather than the flesh of its heart. Forgiveness involves tremendous, sometimes impossible, difficulty. And (perhaps more importantly) demanding or even expecting the victim to forgive raises a nagging, unsettling question about the moral justification of such a demand or expectation. But these are not my reasons. Forgiveness is not the heart but an outer layer because when it is given, if it is given, it is not given in advance, to set the process of reconciliation in motion. It is given within the emerging process, that is, after reconciliation has been established as a goal and the movement toward it has begun. In other words, forgiveness comes after the leap – which I will come to later – has already been taken.

I spoke about the difficulty of forgiveness with D, a physical education and tourism teacher at a school outside Cape Town. A warm, somewhat bearish man, with a boyish face despite his fifty-some years, he's the only one of the school's teachers who talks to his students about the apartheid years and the struggle against it. It's interesting to note that as part of the rejection of the apartheid narrative, history textbooks were naturally also discarded, but as D explains: "New ones have not yet been written," and teaching about the fight against apartheid is not a compulsory part of school curricula. One must add here that the impressive historical museums dealing with apartheid are out of reach for a large part of the poor population, that is, those most affected by apartheid. On the walls of D's classroom are newspaper clippings and quotes from significant figures in the struggle for equality, and the pride with which he talks about his own part in it testifies to his emotional investment both then and now. He sees himself as a product of apartheid and a product of the struggle against it. These left their mark on him – in the opportunities he had (or rather, didn't have), in his choices, in his personality, and in his worldview. No matter how you look at it, after more than two decades without apartheid, D still does not see himself as separate from it.

"I started high school the year the Soweto riots broke out," he said, and this was the headline that framed everything else he told me. "We closed the schools, and for six months we didn't study. We were children, and we roamed the streets in a terrible rage. We broke windows of white-owned shops, I broke them too, and I didn't care whose store it was, as long as it was *white*. I didn't know what to do with all my frustration."

D shifted uncomfortably on the bench we were sitting on together, in a yard devoid of toys, vegetation, or play structures. He seemed to be trying to find a position in which he would be less aware of some large, solid mass that was sitting inside his body and causing him discomfort.

"I had dreams . . . but my life, *all* of our lives, were without freedom. Without *options*. The same story repeated itself when I went to university. That was in the 1980s, and there were serious riots and a lot of violence and again long strikes and suspended studies and lots, *lots* of riots."

D paused for a moment and exhaled the air from his lungs in a loud, slow, very charged exhalation.

"It's been better since '94. There's still discrimination, but we're moving in the right direction," he said, as if trying to calm himself down.

"And what did you do with all that anger?" I asked. "Is it gone? Do you feel inside that you've forgiven?"

D looked around with his emotional brown eyes. He twisted the hairs of his mustache between two fingers as if trying to gather his thoughts, or perhaps his strength, whatever he needed to overcome the ever so slight, yet noticeable, stutter that marked the beginning of all his sentences.

"This was very, *very* difficult," he finally answered, and again his body squirmed next to me on the bench. "I'll tell you the truth, I personally didn't think it was *possible* to forgive. But Papa Mandela spoke to us. Over and over again he spoke to us and explained to us the importance of forgiveness. To forgive for ourselves, to forgive because it was *the right thing* to do. It was very, very difficult, but we listened. *I* listened. And slowly I understood. Maybe not completely, because I'm still trying to understand and there are moments . . . I'm still working on it, still listening to the voice of Papa Mandela inside me."

The difficulty with forgiveness stems at least in part from the fact that unlike empathy – which, like a gaze, is inexhaustible, since people can scatter their gazes in all directions without fear of being left impoverished by all this looking – forgiveness is seen not only as a moral or philosophical position. Forgiveness is an act, and as such, it has a beginning, a duration of some kind, and an end. Although it is possible to forgive repeatedly, it will not necessarily be in response to the same act or have the same recipient. In fact, forgiveness has an element of ownership: it belongs to the person who was hurt, and he can – if he chooses to do so – grant it to the person who hurt him. However, once he has granted it, it is no longer his; it belongs to the other person. In other words, when one forgives, one gives something up, which is in no way a simple thing to.

Indeed, in the context of reconciliation, forgiveness is seen as currency, something traded in exchange for something else – accepting responsibility, for example. Even when forgiveness is at the top of the pyramid of noble deeds, even when it is the moral, right thing to do, it still depends on something – the severity of the act for which the victim is asked to forgive, for example. But is there no limit? Are there actions for which no one has the right to ask forgiveness?

J, a researcher at the University of Rwanda, spoke with me about the moral dimensions of demanding or expecting forgiveness. I previously mentioned our conversation about humans' ability to learn from history and the implicit tension between her, a Tutsi, and H, a Hutu.

"Forgiveness is not something that can be talked about without talking about the *thing* that needs to be forgiven," she stated. As she spoke, she looked at me with piercing eyes, though her voice and body language remained measured and reserved, befitting the restrained, accepting tone that characterizes the society in which she lives. "A woman who was infected with HIV during the genocide, and will continue to live with it for the rest of her life and probably die from it, can you ask her to forgive? No, I don't think you can," she replied, on the off chance I thought that another answer was possible. "And someone whose private parts were cut off," she continued, but then narrowed her eyes and momentarily stopped speaking. "Do you *understand* what that means? It means she has a *hole* instead of a part. Can you expect her to forgive? No, I don't think anyone has the *right* to ask her to forgive. We must let her *be*."

We must let her be. J's words continue to echo inside me. I desire to believe – to paraphrase the words of Aharon Barak, the one-time chief justice of Israel's supreme court, who stated that everything can be judged, that is, everything can be brought before the law – that everything is potentially forgivable. But when I pose the question to myself, there are situations in which I find, like J, that a wall suddenly rises up within me. This wall stands in the way of forgiveness, refusing to let it pass.

I do exercises with myself: I imagine myself into the terrible, horrible situations people shared with me (and I know that my ability to do so, as someone who has not actually experienced them, is limited) and ask myself if I could forgive them in the context of reconciliation. In other words, if I knew that although my forgiveness were not the one thing that would bring about reconciliation, it might contribute something to it, would this allow me to forgive what in any other context would be unforgivable? I'm not sure I'm capable of standing behind my own desire to believe that everything can be forgiven.

Because to answer that I have to think about myself and my end point – my children – and there I find only silence. There I find that I cannot answer the question, that I cannot think of words to express my deepest, most nullifying fear. In the most concrete sense, my consciousness is blocked off there.

"Maybe you can't understand it until you've been through it," G told me at an orphanage near Kigali. And maybe he's right, because people have coped with horrors they never thought they could cope with. But it seems to me that it's not just a matter of the difficulty of imagining a situation I've never experienced, but the difficulty of imagining something that defies logic. It's hard to grasp a circular triangle, it's hard to grasp the loss of a child.

You see, I've been preoccupied with this thing that defies reason, been orbiting this extreme point, since long before I even knew how to define it. In the first years of my life there were three of us: my mother, me, and her violent, clutching fear of losing me. This was a very tangible fear, the boundaries of which exceeded even that of the most anxious mothers. It exceeded reality as well: my mother's anxiety had the presence of a pain that she had already experienced in the past and continued to experience in the present. This was not just a pain that might, possibly, be experienced in the future. When I looked into my mother's eyes, I saw myself dead in them, and I saw her infinite pain in them, a pain that surpassed any sense of sorrow I could feel for my imagined death. Even today, I can revive this feeling within me with the same ease as I can revive a smell that takes me far into the past – a dry, pungent smell that spilled through the car window, from the days when there was no air conditioning and people drove with their windows down, and it hit you in the face as you approached Jerusalem; or a damp, zesty smell that stung your nostrils when the plane door opened at Ben Gurion Airport, back when citrus trees grew not far from it.

But it is not to my mother's anxiety that I go when I imagine my end point. Although the smell remains, reality trumps any imagined danger, and when I imagine this place I find myself facing my grandmother, the mother of my uncle, who was my childhood friend and partner in the secret camp of those he and I called the "normals" (an exclusive camp that included only him and me, of course), a camp that was our fortress when we found ourselves in the frequent storms of those we called – arrogant children that we were – the "crazies" (meaning the rest of the family). More than four decades have passed since he was killed at the end of yet another unnecessary war. When I look into my grandmother's intense, beautiful eyes – even now, when I look into them in my mind's eye – I cringe with grief at her unimaginable, logic-defying loss. I feel guilty about my own, overwhelming, intoxicating relief, the relief that comes from knowing that I am not that mother, but she is.

In fact, the only thing I can imagine with relative clarity when I think about the place my grandmother found herself in is a powerful desire to be given an exemption. A powerful desire to make it clear to everyone that such a blatant oxymoron as a parent losing her child, such a flaw in the order of the world, should not be forgiven by anyone. Because what are you even talking about. Because how could you even consider such a thing.

MORE THAN TWO DECADES after surviving the Gurs, Bergen-Belsen, and Auschwitz concentration camps, Jean Améry wrote in his book *Jenseits von Schuld und Sühne* (Beyond Guilt and Atonement) about forgiveness through its opposite: resentment. More precisely, he wrote about the victim's right to hold on to resentment as an act of protest against the progress of time, which heals wounds, and against reconciliation, which requires looking toward the future. The only possible moral position, for Améry, is to demand the impossible: the abolition of time. That is, to demand that victims and victimizers be confined to the past – which they shared, in contrast to the future – where the victimizers are let out from their corners, and the victims are forced, under immoral social pressure, to forgive and forget. And to those who are disturbed by this resentment – "the chorus of voices calling from all sides for peace, who joyfully propose: Let us not look back, but forward, to a better future, a shared future!" – Améry asks that they be patient.

In terms of the reconciliation process, Améry demands the victim's right to remain at the station of revealing the truth and not proceed from there to the next. As mentioned, forgiveness, when given, is offered in the face of the specific wrong that was inflicted on the victim and is weighed against it. In this sense, forgiveness is a later station that, in order to be reached, requires returning to the wrong in order to look at it, revive it, and make it visible in the public sphere. This is a stage where the victim's testimony carries great weight, and his voice possesses moral force. However, that is but a stage in the process, and this is precisely what Améry rebels against. At some point the reconciling society has exhausted its time at this station and seeks to move on. In this regard, commemoration is an attempt to provide a solution to this difficulty. It expresses a position that goes something like this: we don't forget, we hold ceremonies and erect monuments and museums to tell the story of the injustices of the past. Commemoration allows the process to move forward by marking the past in the present and the future. However, it also replaces the victim's voice, making it redundant. After all, the memory, certainly that which is traumatic, continues in the victim as a living, breathing experience, while that which is immortalized – in images, in words, in monuments – loses some of its vitality, turns flat, is less breathing and alive, as it becomes public property, that is, in the hands of others. The wrongs inflicted on the victim continue to exist within them, detached from advancing time, in a continuous and lonely present, which is difficult even to communicate. Commemoration removes such wrongs from this private space and places them within a context – a matter that raises its own difficulty, which I will address in my discussion of narrative – and turns them into mere building blocks of this larger process. Continuity, the movement that exists in the process, stands in sharp contrast, perhaps too sharp, with the experience of a victim, who remains in his pain, who continues to live it in the present and will continue to live it in the future.

Patience, Améry asks. How much patience? I imagine my grandmother again, and discover that the answer is clear: endless patience. As much as they want. Forgiveness is desirable and noble, but it belongs to the victims; it is theirs, and they can be allowed to do with it as they wish. Reconciliation can exist, or at least begin, without it.

There is also an aesthetic aspect to relocating forgiveness from the realm of necessity to the realm of choice: a reconciliation that does not involve fanfare and trumpets, a reconciliation that acknowledges the pain that has no remedy, a reconciliation that is able to contain such pain within itself, a humble reconciliation appropriate for a painful conflict.

A Layer That Is a Hot Potato: Responsibility

Responsibility illuminates the other side of forgiveness, which is how much forgiveness the party accepting responsibility is willing to grant to behaviors on the victim's side that are a result of the suffering inflicted on him during the conflict, behaviors that in any other context would be unacceptable. However, I bring up this aspect of forgiveness here rather than in the previous section because it is closer to and in fact a corollary of responsibility. This is a sensitive and charged issue that has the potential to be a stumbling block in the reconciliation process, because it gives expression to the deepest longings of the parties involved in the conflict. The victim longs for the recognition that he deserves. In his view, this recognition includes the submission of the victimizer, who accepts, without reservations or excuses, guilt for the injustice that he himself caused or that was caused on his behalf. On the other hand, the victimizer desires recognition of the unique situation that, according to him, turned him into a victimizer. To be more precise, he hopes for a reprieve. Because he had no choice, because he didn't know, etc. There are many other more or less extenuating circumstances, but regardless, they all aim, in their essence, to circumvent the submission that the victim requests as proof of the victimizer's admission that he caused an injustice.

This meeting between the deep – and oppositional – longings of the two parties inevitably makes this a fraught matter. It grows even more fraught as the relationship between the victim's side and the victimizer's side becomes more complex, that is, less black and white. And even more as one moves away from the immediate circle of perpetrators and victims – where it is easier to identify the act and the parties involved – until the question arises as to whether simply belonging to the victimizing group is enough to bear responsibility for the wrongs done in its name. Added to this complexity is the matter of ownership and the act this calls for, that is, the concessions required from all those involved. In other words, in the same way that forgiveness belongs to the victim and it is difficult, and perhaps impossible, to force him to grant it to his victimizer, so responsibility and what stems from it – willingness to forgive victims for behavior caused by their victimization – belongs to the victimizer. And so it is difficult, if not impossible, to force him to give this to his victim.

S, whom I mentioned earlier, spoke to me about such forgiveness. She is the white woman who grew up on a family farm in South Africa, near the border with Zimbabwe, in the protective bubble established by her father, a devout Christian who believed in the equality of all human beings regardless of who they are. She's the one who told me, "I didn't even *know* there was apartheid. I mean, I knew that beyond our farm, which was really something of a bubble, blacks were treated worse than whites. But I didn't *really* know. I didn't know *how much* worse. I think my father tried to protect us," she said sadly, "I think he didn't want us to know that there was such evil in the world."

S didn't really know about apartheid growing up, that is, she didn't know the extent of this oppressive and discriminatory system. But she could have known, had she insisted, and since she realized this, she has dedicated her life to fixing what can be fixed, or rather: what she is able to fix. She isn't merely atoning for her ignorance. She recognizes that, as a white person who lived in South Africa during the apartheid years, she is responsible for the wrongs committed by the white population against the nonwhite population. The fact that she never supported the apartheid regime has no bearing on her responsibility or on the privileges she has had in her life simply by being white.

She is a math and science teacher in an especially depressed and difficult area, that is, an area where many black, few colored, and zero white people live. She is a social activist in the nearby township, where most of her students live, where she helps parents organize so that they have the strength to face the drug dealers who coax their children into doing drugs.

"You can't imagine how much power it gives them when they stand together in front of the dealers," she said. "Do you see this neighborhood?" S pointed to a cluster of tin shacks on both sides of a dirt path. "We succeeded there. The parents stand there in shifts. Most of them don't have jobs anyway, so it also gives them something to do. They stand outside and keep the dealers from coming, and it works!" She added with emotion, "The dealers have gone elsewhere!"

In her small car, S took me to visit the huge township where tin shacks, close together, stretch far into the distance, like an ocean whose edge merges into the sky. S noticed that my gaze lingered for a moment on a woman hanging laundry on clotheslines stretched between a fence and posts in her tiny yard, white laundry on one string, colored on another.

"Yes, it's heart-rending," she said, picking up on my feelings. The human need for beauty – even where lives are dominated by poverty, misery, and a lack of hope – never ceases to amaze me.

S went on to say that many of these houses are clean and tidy inside, even though there is no running water in them, and that you can find a touch of care in them. A flower that someone picked and placed in a glass, for example.

In the township, where in addition to poverty, misery, and a lack of hope, there is also a very high level of crime and violence. S spends time here because she is known and accepted by the members of the community, but for the most part, no white people are to be found here. At night, drivers will take long detours to avoid approaching these areas, to avoid even passing by their outskirts.

"These children were born free," S explains when I ask her about her sense of personal security. A sense that, it seems, she disregards defiantly, as if reminding herself that this lack of security is one of the places where she pays a personal price. And that's a good thing, because being white, she should pay a personal price. "They don't know how bad it was before. They only know how bad it is for them now. They see that whites have cars and jobs and bigger houses. And they have a lot of anger in their hearts. But if you look, most violence is the violence of theft. That means it's the violence of survival, and that's understandable, because they're in a situation of survival. It's not their fault, it's the fault of apartheid and everything that it took from them, and it's the fault of those who allowed apartheid to exist. They need to be helped. They should be *forgiven*. This is our task and this is the price we as a society must pay, must pay until they can be rehabilitated."

S expresses, on a daily basis, her willingness to accept personal responsibility for the injustices of apartheid simply because she is a white woman who grew up and lived under it. Her willingness can be seen in the life she chooses to live, and in her worldview as well. Hers is one in which she essentially suspends all criticism of South Africa's nonwhite population. She presents a forgiving attitude toward their weaknesses, a forgiveness similar to that which is required for the less admirable behaviors of a child who has suffered from abuse. All of this requires a kind of submission that not many are capable of. De Klerk, for example, who was the last president of the apartheid regime and who effectively brought it to an end, refused to acknowledge his personal responsibility for the injustices of the apartheid regime he headed. De Klerk spoke of apartheid in terms of a political mistake, not a moral failure. He insisted – even during the Truth and Reconciliation Commission hearings – that the leaders of apartheid, the same people who were the devil incarnate in the eyes of nonwhite South Africans, were "good and honorable" people. De Klerk had the greatness and power to understand that the apartheid regime had lost its right to exist. Moreover, in his negotiations with Nelson Mandela he put into practice the meaning of reconciliation as a redefinition of relationship. Still, he did not reveal within himself the generosity, humility, and perhaps even integrity that were required of him to grant the victims the submission that they sought. Many found, then and now, his position a tough one to swallow, yet it did not prevent the reconciliation process from taking shape and taking place. Accepting personal responsibility was not necessary.

The question of responsibility is a difficult one. It is also very personal, as it concerns one's self-perception. More precisely, it concerns the extent to which one experiences oneself as part of the society in which one lives, and therefore bears responsibility for what happens, or does not happen, in it. This question also forces people to define their circles of affiliation – does their commitment begin and end with themselves, their home, and their nuclear family, or does it extend to their extended family, their community, their workplace, their city, their country, their nation, or their religion? Or perhaps their commitment actually has no boundaries, and applies to all human beings.

Sometimes this sense of responsibility is somewhat vague, such as what I felt as a white woman in Africa and especially in Rwanda, where – unlike South Africa – all white people are foreigners. I myself was not a British, French, Belgian, German, or Portuguese colonialist in Africa. And, as far as I know, neither were any of my ancestors. Nevertheless, I cringed uncomfortably while living among the locals. Not because of the physically challenging conditions, which were beyond anything I was familiar with back home, but because I was white. That is, because I belong to the victimizers, if only through the benefits I derived from the very fact of being born into a society where the possibilities are also a result of colonialism, which depleted the African continent's resources and corrupted its social fabric.

Sometimes this sense of responsibility is more explicit and leads to action, like the one that led me to engage with the possibility of reconciliation and to write this book. More precisely, it is the knowledge that as an Israeli and a Jew living in Israel, I am part of the conflict, part of those who suffer from its existence but also profit from it, and part of those who will have to be held accountable and pay its price. At the same time, I must admit that I also experience ambivalence, the difficulty of silently and humbly accepting full responsibility. I am forced to acknowledge that other, less generous voice speaking within me. A somewhat whiny voice that seeks recognition that I am one of those who is working for equal rights, for justice, and for an end to the occupation and the conflict. It is unreasonable, the voice nags, it's totally not fair! It's not fair that I should be associated with those who think that the conflict is insoluble or that the price of resolving it is unacceptable. This is not the group that I want to see myself as a part of.

Despite this voice, it seems to me that the white South African cartoonist Zapiro captures my sentiment regarding my own sense of responsibility:

6

The Heart

With Less Than This, It Won't Work

At the heart of reconciliation is a recognition that both parties to the conflict will continue to exist in the same shared space, that their rights in and over it are equal, and that therefore the future and character of this shared space will have to be determined collaboratively, and equally.

That's it.

And yet in the context of conflict this is as difficult as recognition gets, because such recognition must create itself out of the patterns produced by the conflict, patterns that by their very nature do not allow ideas that undermine them to take shape and come into existence. And this is as difficult as recognition gets, because if it nevertheless succeeds in creating itself, then it threatens everything that is known and familiar to the self that recognizes it, including everything that is known and familiar to this very self about itself. In other words, it is a recognition that means, at the deepest level, a readiness to change, and it seems to me that few things are as threatening as change. And not least of all, it is as difficult as recognition gets for us Israelis, because it has practical consequences that are frightening to think about. I'm speaking here of everything from the definition of the state and its future image to the renunciation of the privileges that we, as Israeli Jews, have become accustomed to seeing as our natural rights.

Everything else comes later, and this is part of the enormous difficulty that the heart of reconciliation poses: it must be thought of in isolation from the context of its future components – truth, justice, repair, responsibility, forgiveness, empathy. These are components that will gradually develop in its wake, but at its birth they are absent and may even seem impossible. In fact, from the perspective of the conflict-produced patterns that we Israelis are all prisoners of to one degree or another, this recognition makes no sense and certainly cannot be justified using the language of the conflict. Therefore, to reach it, the heart of reconciliation requires something we are not used to doing, most certainly not in this context: taking a leap of faith.

Yeshayahu Leibovitz – the Israeli Orthodox Jewish philosopher, public intellectual, and outspoken critic of Israeli society – spoke of the leap of faith a person must take to become a believer. For him, faith – in God, for example – has no rational basis, meaning it is not something that can be deduced from a process of thinking about one thing that leads into another. It is a decision, and whoever decides that this is what he wants must jump over this wall of illogicality. And yet when he lands in the space of faith, he will find himself in a world full of logic.

However, one does not have to go so far as faith. Some scientific theories are also accepted as axiomatic despite the fact that essential parts of them are still missing, that is, no proof for them has been found. As I was writing these lines, the world was informed that proof of the existence of gravitational waves had been discovered. One hundred years after Einstein's theory of general relativity was postulated and accepted, the world received proof of the existence of one of its critical components. In the hundred years preceding this discovery, its existence was assumed, and the absence of proof did not detract from the coherence of the larger theory. In other words, the place of this component was marked out and the entire theory awaited it without its larger internal logic being compromised by its absence.

Similarly, reconciliation is a completely different way of thinking than conflict. It employs a different logic. Consider for a moment Wittgenstein's statement about the difference between 2+2=5 and 2+2=97. The logic of conflict is not only unable to justify the leap toward reconciliation, it is a leap from a known and coherent place to a place where there are no anchors, since this alternative logic – that of reconciliation – does not yet exist: It is this very leap of faith that creates the logic of reconciliation. This leap also draws out the place of those future elements of reconciliation that, once created, will become its anchors. This leap of faith possesses an additional and very profound meaning, because it finds one taking ownership of time. In the simplest sense, one signals the following as one leaps: what was is not what will be.

Who Is an Authentic Reconciler (And How Do We Recognize Them)

A person who apologizes from the bottom of his heart does not look or sound like someone who makes a tactical or manipulative apology. Along similar lines, love is evident in the person who loves, not in the one who makes empty declarations of love. But in an environment saturated with mixed messages and emotional manipulation, we may lose confidence in our ability to identify who is sincere and whose intentions are hidden. Similarly, in places where hopeful concepts such as "reconciliation" and "peace" have been eroded and the messages conveyed in the discussion about them are vague or ambiguous, there is a pervasive distrust that leads to fatalistic thinking (everyone is a liar and no one can be trusted) and passivity (so what I do doesn't make a difference). Supposedly, there is nothing simpler than setting reconciliation as a goal. Most Israelis and even a large set of Israeli politicians would say that they strive for it. However, it seems to me that one disturbing sign (among many) of the lack of hope here is the way the very concept of "reconciliation" has been degraded. We are at the point where it is difficult to tell who is really striving for it and who is doing little more than paying lip service in order to appease their own consciences and those of their voters. Meanwhile, their actions – to borrow from one of the leaders of the South African opposition during the apartheid era, Frederick van Zyl Slabbert – are like rearranging deck chairs on the Titanic. The rule that if it looks like a duck and sounds like a duck then it probably is a duck loses its relevance in a situation where we are surrounded by the sights and sounds of ducks originating from duck impersonators. In this not-so-simple situation we lose our trust in our own intuition, which is one of the important tools at our disposal when it comes to identifying authenticity.

The attempt to characterize the authentic reconciler requires a few more words, since contrary to what one might expect, there isn't complete overlap between authenticity and a necessary corresponding emotion. To put it bluntly, the corresponding emotion – the one that, according to the logic of most of us, should be the generator and engine of the reconciler and that, for most of us, is something taken from the world of flower children – is not necessary. Just as empathy, forgiveness, and responsibility are not the heart of reconciliation but its outer layers, so the emotional affect expected – and perhaps even hoped for – from the authentic reconciler is not obligatory. In fact, when we come to search within ourselves and around us for the authentic reconciler, what we must look for is seriousness, a quality that can stem from a decision, can originate in the head. The heart can join in later. Therefore, the question that should guide the search for the authentic reconciler is: Who has come to do the work? In other words, who has established reconciliation as a goal and developed a plan to work toward it?

I would like to propose a question that will be a kind of litmus test for verifying the authenticity of those politicians who claim to speak in favor of reconciliation. This test can be applied in much the same way among those who are interested in ascertaining for themselves whether and to what extent their desire for reconciliation is genuine:

What needs to happen for reconciliation to occur?

This question is an open one, that is, it places few limits on possible answers. But it does, nonetheless, assume reconciliation as a goal, if only for the purpose of the discussion. As such, it requires the respondents to produce *some* statement regarding reconciliation. In this way, it places a mirror – sometimes too well-lit and thus unflattering – up to the respondents and displays their attitude toward the possibility of reconciliation.

An authentic person is one whose mouth and heart are aligned and therefore has no need for quibbles, digressions, and double-speak. Hence, one of the characteristics of authenticity is simplicity (as opposed, of course, to simplification). This is evident, among other things, in language, and more precisely, in its structure and not necessarily in its content, which, as mentioned, can easily be manipulated. Indeed, if we return for a moment to language, we find that it can offer a tangible means for locating this simplicity.

Israeli discourse, judging by the answers prevalent in it, fails the simplicity test when it comes to language that characterizes authenticity. The most obvious expression of this is that for the most part we do not talk about reconciliation. We used to talk about "peace," then we moved on to "agreement," while today "conflict management" has become a common expression that is accepted with indifference. And in places where reconciliation (oops, my bad – peace or agreement) is still mentioned, the discussion is always accompanied by the addition of "but." This ungainly conjunction annihilates what comes before it, by disrupting the balance in the sentence and shifting the emphasis from the *supposed* subject of the sentence to what is *supposedly* nothing more than an addition meant to clarify. To be more precise, it is not the actual use of "but" that is problematic, but rather the manner in which it is used, that is, what "but" serves to undermine. Those who are sincere in their desire for reconciliation may also speak of "but," but in their case the use of the word is reversed. Such people use it to challenge the rhetoric that emphasizes the difficulties of reconciliation. For example: The costs of reconciliation are high, but the costs of war are even higher.

Here's a taste of the discourse prevalent in the place I call home:

We strive for reconciliation, *but* one that will ensure the existence of Israel as a Jewish state.

Even if we assume that we are indeed "striving" – that is, we are active and not just passively "willing" – this is not exactly a heartwarming invitation to our interlocutors. In addition (and this is a bonus for parts of the Israeli public), such language is an affront to Palestinian citizens of Israel, who are excluded from the conversation about possible solutions to the Israeli-Palestinian conflict. After all (so the thinking goes), they are not flesh and blood of the Jewish state, and therefore cannot possibly take part in determining its fate. Israel has come a long way since it was first conceived as a "state of the Jews," a framework that could have been democratic and could have included non-Jewish citizens with equal rights. But it became a "Jewish state," a political framework in some ways resembling the "Islamic state" of Iran after the Khomeini Revolution.

We strive for reconciliation, *but* one that will ensure our security.

Why, in fact, is it necessary to state the obvious? Is this something that needs to be said when it comes to a state of reconciliation, a state that is the opposite of war? This seemingly superfluous statement, however, is far from accidental; it is not just a bunch of unnecessary words. It reflects a clear mark of the Israeli-Jewish mindset. This particular "but" demonstrates the deep distrust of many Israelis toward Palestinians, even post-conflict Palestinians. This is nothing more than a so-called willingness for reconciliation that implicitly communicates: We do not believe that you are capable of seeing us as anything but enemies.

We strive for reconciliation, *but* one in which our enemies will recognize our rights.

Again, why is it necessary to state the obvious? Is it really possible to reconcile with someone – not just sign an agreement, but reconcile – without recognizing them and their rights?

These kinds of clumsy messages are the hallmarks of those who use words like "reconciliation" and "peace" cynically. Their words point not to the goal but rather to what makes it unobtainable.

It is also worth paying attention to their tone. The responses of those for whom reconciliation is nothing more than an empty slogan sound like they are setting a precondition, making a demand, and sometimes even issuing a threat. Whatever they're doing, it does not sound like they're offering up an invitation.

Here is a viable proposed answer: For reconciliation to occur, both sides need to conceive together, imagine together, their common and equal future, with mutual recognition of the traumas of the past, the anxieties in the present, and the hopes for the future.

The inauthentic formulations have an additional common denominator, a characteristic that is the easiest to identify and therefore perhaps the one that is most worth focusing on: they concern only the needs and sensitivities of the speaker's side, the Israeli side in this case. And they condition reconciliation on what the opposing side, that is, the Palestinians, should do (prevent terrorism, recognize our historical or national rights, etc.) or should not do (incite against us, work to achieve recognition in international institutions, etc.). At the same time, they completely ignore what the Israeli side should or should not do, as if reconciliation were a prize that Israel might (or might not) give to the Palestinians if they earn (from Israel, of course) a good grade for meeting (Israel's, of course) standards. As a very useful rule of thumb, grading the opposing side (are they a partner or not, are they serious or not, are they strong enough or not strong enough to make decisions) is another warning light when it comes to detecting authenticity.

So who is the authentic reconciler? And more precisely (and optimistically), what is that place in a person whose yearning for reconciliation is authentic?

This person – whether he's a politician or not – is the one whose answer resonates somehow with the heart of reconciliation. In other words, how do they answer the question: What needs to happen for there to be reconciliation? Those for whom reconciliation is a goal – even if they have established it as such for pragmatic rather than principled reasons – will give answers that contain the foundations of equal rights and full participation, without reservations and without hesitation.

I propose a possible answer here, and an invitation to you, the reader, to examine whether it is an answer you can live with:

For reconciliation to occur, both sides must recognize that they will forever continue to live together in this land, that their rights in and over it are equal, and that the future and character of the land will be shaped jointly, in a way that will ensure the rights, dignity, and physical and mental well-being of all.

How does that feel?

And When It Happens Here, and There Is No Doubt It Will, What Will It Look Like?

A bold heading like this begs an explanation. Well, discriminatory and oppressive regimes eventually disappear. I invite anyone who doubts whether the State of Israel discriminates against Palestinian citizens of Israel and oppresses Palestinians who live under its occupation in the West Bank and Gaza to ask themselves the following simple and very concrete questions: Can the "other" – that is, the Palestinian man or woman, boy or girl – realize his or her talents and dreams? Is there anything the Israeli Jews have done that prevents them from doing so? Since the answer to the first question can only be no and the answer to the second can only be yes, I would like to quote here the words of Martin Luther King Jr.: "I am absolutely convinced that the system of segregation is on its deathbed today, and the only thing uncertain is how costly the segregationists will make the funeral."[1] And for the benefit of those who find the positive answer to be reasonable, for those not embarrassed by a discriminatory and oppressive Israel, I would like to quote more of King's words: "Injustice anywhere is a threat to justice everywhere. We are caught in an inescapable network of mutuality, tied in a single garment of destiny. Whatever affects one directly, affects all indirectly."

A study of the reconciliation processes of South Africa and Rwanda leaves us with two certainties and one unknown. The certainties: reconciliation is possible; and it will be accompanied by great pain. The unknown: we do not know what the picture of reconciliation will look like; all we know is that it is likely to look different from what most of us imagine, and different from that of South Africa and Rwanda. All that aside, we do know some of what will happen at the beginning of the process and some of what will happen during it.

I'll start from the end: it is impossible to know what the shape of this reconciliation will be. Not only because, as the Talmudic phrase goes, prophecy is for fools, but because it is a shape that cannot be crafted alone. Any attempt to devise a solution to the Israeli-Palestinian conflict without the full and equal participation of the Palestinian side (those inside the Green Line and those in the occupied territories) would be the mother of all mistakes made by Israeli-Jewish society. We, Jewish Israelis, insist on negotiating among ourselves about the nature of the solution we desire – two states, one state (apartheid or a state of all its citizens), two states under one federation – without taking into account, without *truly* taking into account, that there is another side. This kind of discussion is nothing more than another expression of Israeli-Jewish society's deep corruption and perhaps the clearest sign that it is trapped within its conflict-produced patterns of consciousness: it is a society that does not think in terms of cooperation. This is a society that oscillates between the foolishly arrogant assumption that it

1 Speech at Pennsylvania State University, January 21, 1965.

understands – that it is capable of understanding – the needs, sensitivities, and positions of the Palestinians, and the denial of their very legitimacy.

However, a thing or two can be known about the reconciliation process: it will be bloody, it will be difficult, and it will be filled with ambiguity. It will be *bloody*, because from the moment reconciliation is signaled as a goal, everyone who is threatened by the possibility of reconciliation will do everything, absolutely everything, to sabotage it. And every time such people succeed, the choice of reconciliation will be put to the test once again.

It will be *difficult*, because it will force those involved in it to give up on quite a few fantasies – starting with those about what reconciliation is and, no less important, is not, continuing with the sense of precedence Israeli Jews have regarding this land, and ending with the fantasy of the partner, including the leaders, they would like to find on the other side. On this note, I would like to draw attention to Mohandas Gandhi and Martin Luther King Jr. Each led a nonviolent struggle, which should have been the kind of struggle their oppressors could only dream about. And yet, those whom Gandhi and King fought against – the British in India and white segregationists in the United States – did not exactly embrace them.

It will be *ambiguous*, because the process will force those involved to encounter the "other" and his narrative. This encounter will inevitably undermine the comfortable and comforting victimhood of all parties in our conflict. Indeed, one of the most distinct and ironic characteristics of this conflict is the similarity between the two parties, both of whom see themselves as victims, experience themselves as more vulnerable than their opponent, and feel a strong need for the other party to acknowledge this. "You love this place and express your love for the same plants, the same herbs, as if you were me. As if you were speaking on my behalf. And that is the power of literature. There is an intersection between writings about this landscape in Hebrew poetry and Arabic poetry. Several Israeli poets express my attitude toward the landscape in poems that I would sign myself. . . . It is our fate that we settle and dwell in the same metaphor."[2] These are the words of the Palestinian poet Mahmoud Darwish, who touched the sensitive area of conflicting narratives that nevertheless share many of the same building blocks.

It is enough to say the word "narrative" – which is as essential to humans as air but is also a magnet for projections – and the hackles of all involved are raised. It's not hard to understand why. It's a bag of explosives: Who was here first, Jews or Palestinians? Whose attachment to the land is older? Is Zionism colonialist? Or did it become corrupted by its occupation of the Palestinian territories? And who started the conflict? Was it the Zionists, or was it the Palestinians who didn't accept the 1947 UN Partition Plan? And who is to blame for the situation of the Palestinians? Is it again the Zionists, or is it perhaps those Arab landowners who, during the British Mandate, sold their lands to the Zionists and abandoned the tenants who worked them? Or is it perhaps the Arab countries that have repeatedly turned their backs on the Palestinians? Do the settlers alone bear the responsibility for the occupation, or is it the responsibility of the entire Israeli-Jewish public that has allowed them to do as they please? And what was the starting point of the conflict – 1948 or 1967? The enormous difficulty in creating – or perhaps it would be more accurate to say quilting – a shared narrative whose blanket could cover and keep warm both sides of the conflict can be seen in the gap between black and white experience in the United States. In her book *Regarding the Pain of Others*, Susan Sontag draws attention to the absence – at the time she wrote the book, in 2003 – of a museum commemorating the history of black slavery. Though it was 133 years since slavery was abolished by law, not a single museum had been established to tell the story of this grim chapter in American history, Sontag writes, explaining (but not excusing) this

---

2 Quoted in Helit Yeshurun, *How Did You Do It?* Hakibbutz Hameuchad, 2016 (Hebrew).

implausible reality by asserting that this memory is perceived as having the power to endanger social stability.

What the meeting of narratives will do for the Palestinian side, namely, the questions they will ask themselves and the psychological processes they will go through, I will leave to the Palestinians. That is theirs. As for our side, that of Israeli-Jewish society, the encounter with the Palestinian narrative will pose difficult questions to us that concern the basis of our existence as Jews in Israel and the price that the Palestinians have paid and are still paying for it. In other words, these are questions that will confront us with both the Zionist fantasy and the Zionist reality, both of which can be considered by a brief reading of a couple poems by Nathan Alterman. Alterman – who, in addition to poetry, wrote plays and essays – was a leader in Hebrew poetry's avant-garde movement, a spokesman for the Israeli national struggle, and a public intellectual with wide-ranging interests.

In "Morning Song" (1934), also known as "We Love You, Homeland," Alterman depicts in heroic, romantic terms the difficulty endured by Jews during the pre-state period due to challenges posed by the land itself ("The desert – we shall carve a path through it / The swamps – we shall drain them") and violence inherent in the national project ("If the road is difficult and treacherous / And even if some fall in battle"). But such difficulties are wrapped in a commitment to the Zionist project of building a state and a passionate love for the land. In line with the collective culture of the time, the speaker in the poem is the collective "we," while the addressee is the beloved land itself ("We'll clothe you in a dress of concrete and cement / And spread carpets of gardens for you . . . We'll love you forever, homeland, / We're yours in battle and toil!").

"About This" (1948) portrays war crimes committed by Israeli soldiers during the 1948 war. It depicts an Israeli youth ("he smiled with his baby teeth") and an old Palestinian man and woman in a city occupied by Israeli forces. The youth shoots the old man and the woman, and Alterman makes the claim that this is a picture from the battle for our freedom, a battle that demands poems depicting it, but should also demand poems depicting *this*, that is, war crimes ("If then, we shall sing to it about 'delicate incidents' / Whose name, it so happens – is murder . . . Because boys and girls, and we with them, / Some in practice / Some with a pat of consent, / Pushed on with muttering 'necessity' and 'vengeance,' / To the realm of war criminals.")

Some have suggested that "About This" is nothing more than an attempt to portray the incident described in that poem as a one-time event, thereby legitimizing other serious war crimes committed during the War of Independence. Nevertheless, this poem opens a crack in the wall of denial that is based on the notion of "there was nothing here, only sand and swamps." It similarly questions the self-image of a society that claims it somehow managed to do the impossible: take part in a war without being corrupted by it.

THE THOUGHT of the next step, that is, what comes after recognizing the other's narrative, or even just parts of it, is one of the heavier and more cumbersome chains that conflict-produced patterns wrap around our ankles. And it acts on us the way anxiety can: by inducing paralysis. However, as can be seen from the cases of South Africa and Rwanda, and as simple logic suggests, there is no single, necessary connection between recognition and action. There are injustices that cannot be remedied without causing new, equally serious injustices, and there are those that cannot be corrected because the laws of nature refuse to cooperate. As Jean Améry writes in *Beyond Guilt and Atonement*: "Even if you return to a physical place, you will never get back the lost time." Splitting apart recognition and action, especially when we view the latter as naturally stemming from the former, is difficult to consider, and even more difficult to accept. Yet it is an inevitable part of the reconciliation process – and at the same time a product of the process and one of the factors that allow it to exist.

For example, a Palestinian recognition that it was the Jews' need to survive, a need perhaps more desperate than any in human history, that drew the Jews to Zionism and led to their determination, however frantic, to establish a state does not oblige the Palestinians to give up their rights in this land, nor does it oblige them to accept with submission the prices they have paid. Similarly, Israeli-Jewish recognition of the price paid by the Palestinians for what, from the Jewish perspective, was the salvation and normalization of the Jewish people, does not oblige Israeli Jews to try to turn back the wheel of time. Just as there is no single, necessary connection between recognizing a wrong and correcting it, there is no single, necessary connection between recognizing the narrative of the other and the practical implications of that recognition. In Darwish's words: "Even if I think your grandfather was an occupier, that doesn't prevent me from recognizing your right to exist. Each of us has an occupier grandfather. Show me one innocent grandfather in history." There are truths that can be combined into a single truth, and there are others that can only exist side by side, even as they exist in contradiction. The process of becoming familiar with each other's narratives will bring up things, probably many things, that the sides involved will be able to see and recognize, even if they can't necessarily accept them. One should not underestimate the enormous difficulty and profound significance of such seeing and recognizing. But these things can only be corrected in relation to the future, that is, only by redefining the relationship between the parties.

But who is to blame? Who should take responsibility? Who should apologize to whom? In other words, who is the bad guy in this story? These are questions that will come up, and it is not certain that we will succeed, even given a reconciliation process, in reaching a unified narrative. Of course, such a narrative would facilitate the work of reconciliation. For those who belong to the "right" group, it would bestow recognition that would serve as a kind of protected space that may ease the act of reconciling. Meanwhile, for each person who belongs to the "guilty" group, such a narrative creates a space in which the steps they must take are marked out for them, and this individual becomes part of a group that shares this moral burden. But like all crude divisions, the one that emerges from a shared but dichotomous narrative does not cover the full range of human experiences, not even in South Africa, where the victim-victimizer dichotomy was taken for granted. A white mother and long-time anti-apartheid activist in South Africa, who lost her daughter in a terrorist act committed by a black resistance organization, belongs – due to her race – to the "guilty" group. At the same time those she must face in the reconciliation process are those responsible for the death of her daughter, who, like her, was an activist for equal rights for black citizens. As a private individual, she is the victim; as a white person, she is the victimizer. And she has to reconcile with those who as black people are the victim and as private individuals are the victimizers.

Is a unified narrative essential to reconciliation? No. More precisely: No, but with a temporal caveat, which I'll offer in a moment. The possibility of two contradictory narratives living side by side and coexisting in a common reconciled space can be seen again in the seemingly "simpler" case of South Africa. There it was clear that black people were the firstborn, original sons and daughters of the country, and white people came to it from Europe and settled there only a few hundred years ago. However, facts are one thing, desires another. The white population of South Africa saw itself as an indigenous South African group. Mandela, who understood the power and significance of subjective identity (for the sake of the discussion, let's put aside for the moment the question of whether there is an identity that is *not* subjective), recognized that white people were indigenous South Africans, sons and daughters of the land with equal rights in and to it. He left aside questions of who arrived first and thus who could claim primacy or precedence. Had he not conceded such matters, the black citizens would have had the upper hand in a knockout. What can we learn from this when it comes to the narrative complexity of the Israeli-Palestinian conflict? Either or both sides can continue to see themselves as the original or firstborn of the land, but they can still join together in that part of the narrative which can be shared: the decision to put aside this question when it comes to anything impacting the future.

In fact, the future is the only part of the narrative on which agreement is essential. So while in the case of our conflict a shared narrative about the past or the present may be oxymoronic, a shared narrative about the future is perfectly possible, and there is nothing about this that contradicts logic. The essence of this shared narrative, which echoes the heart of reconciliation, is the mutual recognition that both parties to the conflict are children of the land, whose common future in the land is a given and whose rights in and over it are equal.

This discussion of the narrative brings us closer to another hot potato: religion, which carries enormous weight in the conflict, so enormous that at times it seems that the very act of dealing with the religious divide will lead to a religious war that could ignite the region and all of us with it. And yet I haven't given religion its own space in this discussion. And for good reason. Religion – any religion – is a human creation. Like a fragrance given off by the body, like a sublime creation of the soul. As such, humans – its creators and rulers – will do with it what their worldview and choices tell them to do with it. In fact, this is what the middle of the reconciliation process, which can last a long time, will demonstrate: everything is subject to choices, and this includes signaling reconciliation as a goal, or choosing not to. And just as outbursts of violence, which will no doubt occur, can equally serve those who want to stop the process and those who continue to strive for it, so too can religion. Those whose worldview is that we will forever live by the sword will seize on the seemingly insoluble dispute over the holy sites, will emphasize the fact that the hawkish parties in our conflict, unlike those in South Africa and Rwanda, are not of the same religion. And they will probably point out that Judaism and Islam lack the emphasis on forgiveness and atonement that is so dominant in Christianity, and which was of great importance in the reconciliation processes in both South Africa and Rwanda.

Yet throughout history, religion has been molded, changed, and adapted to address new situations without eroding its foundations, that is, without threatening what is sacred to its believers. As a human creation, religion contains the full spectrum of human experience, and one can choose to promote those aspects that lead to reconciliation or those that divide. A person who chooses to establish reconciliation as a goal can agree with his friend who attaches special importance to the fact that the hawkish parties in our conflict do not share a common religion. Indeed, a shared religion – Christianity – played an important role in the reconciliation processes in South Africa and Rwanda, and the foundations of forgiveness and atonement had symbolic force and were one of the driving forces of those processes. However, he can also draw his friend's attention to an equally significant matter: under the umbrella of this shared Christian faith, both the atrocities of apartheid in South Africa and the genocide in Rwanda took place. In the latter, there were priests and nuns who took an active part in the killing. Those who choose to establish reconciliation as a goal will emphasize the coexistence and cross-pollination between Jews and Muslims that have existed throughout their shared history. Those who choose to establish reconciliation as a goal will rely on religious sources to emphasize the voices that advocate peace, that prioritize our children's future, or that call for compassion in the treatment of others. Or they will find in these sources a justification for reordering the hierarchy of objects of faith (and in fact, for introducing the hierarchy into places where its existence is taboo), as, for example, Haviva Pedaya does in her article "Mass Psychosis Between the Temple Mount and Facebook." Pedaya both explores and experiences

Jewish tradition, and she emphasizes the religious principle, "A time to act for the Lord, as they have violated your Torah." Put differently: "Sometimes Torah is found in its repudiation," meaning that one can find in Jewish tradition the justification for suspending a halachic law (guarding the Temple Mount, in Pedaya's example) in favor of a supra-halachic law, something more important and more serious (Judaism as a whole and Israel as a sovereign state, in the same example), due to a public emergency (the danger of moral destruction from within and terrorist destruction from without, still in the same example).

I would like to end with the beginning of the reconciliation process and dwell for a moment on what G, a Rwandan lawyer, told me. G took part both in the talks on the Arusha Accords – that effort to regulate relations between the Hutu and Tutsi before the genocide – and in the reconciliation mechanisms after the massacre. In particular, she participated in the writing of the new constitution and the process that allowed the repatriation of many refugees – most of them Hutu, that is, from the "aggressor" side – back to their communities. G herself is a Tutsi who grew up as a refugee in Uganda. The genocide left her a widow with four young children when her husband and the father of her children, an RPF fighter, was killed in a battle with Hutu militias. She also lost her aunt, her mother's sister, who was married to a Hutu man, in the genocide, as well as five of that aunt's children, who were murdered by their brother, also her aunt's son. The father of the family, who was Hutu, had been killed in an accident a few years before the genocide. According to Rwandan tradition, the children were also considered Hutu, but her cousin could not bear what was Tutsi about himself, she explained, that is, everything that came from his mother. So he murdered five of his six brothers and sisters, and their families. One sister managed to escape. Despite his frenzy, he could not bring himself to kill his mother, so he asked another Hutu – a Hutu orphan raised by his mother as her own son – to do it for him. The adopted orphan agreed.

"What error or failure in your reconciliation process would you recommend we learn from?" I asked her.

G thought for a long moment. She closed her eyes tightly for a moment to fight off her tears, then said: "Don't wait as long as we did. Start now."

About this beginning, about what will come even before setting reconciliation as a goal, one thing can be said for sure: it will be the result of a change in our perception of ourselves and our role toward the next generation. The most tangible expression of this change will be a shift in the center of gravity within our collective consciousness, from the past and the present to the future. I'm talking here about a most dramatic shift, for it will require us to recognize that we are the generation of the desert described in Exodus.

The defeatism of this biblical generation prevented it from reaching the Promised Land and was buried along with it in the desert, in part so that this way of being would not be passed on to the next generation. And in a reconciling society, the generation of conflict humbly accepts the difficulties that reconciliation brings with it, difficulties that are sometimes unbearable. In a reconciling society, the desert generation grits its teeth and buries within itself what sometimes defies logic, thus paving the way for the next generation.

The process will begin with the understanding, the readiness, and later the desire to accept what is required of us: to swallow even that which is indigestible and to reconcile – even if this reconciliation contains artificial, incomplete, and imperfect elements – so that our children can grow up into a different reality. And also, perhaps, to correct the terrible distortion that has taken root in our society, in which our children are repeatedly sent to sacrifice their lives for a bloody future instead of their parents taking on the act of sacrifice in the present.

Because isn't the latter the proper order of things?

7

Reconciliation After October Seventh

ONCE, WHEN I WANTED to understand something, think about it, process it, I knew just what to do: invite myself to the desk in my study, in my home, and in my city, and in my language as well. To a space whose protection had been obtained through much work and at great expense, and whose existence had become a constant in my life. Even when I wasn't there, because writing had grown threatening and I needed to give it a break, or because life was pulling me away, I knew at some point that I'd return. To this place that I describe here in a way that situates four spaces, each of which is marked by some kind of border: psychological, architectural, municipal, linguistic (of course it can be described in other ways too). However, the reality after October Seventh is one in which all spaces – physical, mental, verbal – have been violated. It seems that humanity itself has been violated. I write these words from a space that to a large extent no longer exists.

I wrote the book you are holding during the years I worked for the prevention and treatment of malnutrition among impoverished communities in South Africa, Rwanda, Kenya, the Democratic Republic of Congo, Ethiopia, and Uganda. The work there stirred my heart and my conscience, and it occupied my thoughts as well, but it was my encounter with South Africa and Rwanda that, in many ways, felt like a homecoming. I got to know societies that in the recent past were consumed by seemingly endless conflict, yet underwent a transformation and became societies where reconciliation is ever present. Present in discourse, in thought, in public spaces, in emotional life. Present in everything, because at its deepest level, at its essence, reconciliation is the exact opposite of conflict. This presence resembled – in the mode of thinking, of reasoning, in its rhythms and associations – the conversations that took place around the dinner table in the family in which I was raised. My family knew the costs of war intimately and understood peace as a moral imperative, as a collective project of humanity, whose sons and daughters have an obligation to do whatever they can for its sake. And here in South Africa and Rwanda I felt that I was again sitting around the family dinner table on Friday, talking about life and reconciliation, about reconciliation and life, thereby weaving them into a single fabric.

Writing *On Reconciliation* was a journey that began in 2014, following my time in South Africa and Rwanda, with a re-examination and sharpening of my thoughts about the ways and conditions in which conflict ends. It continued with conversations that took place following its publication in Hebrew in 2017, as well as lectures I gave to diverse audiences with varied backgrounds and political views, mainly in Israel but not only. The ideas that I put forward in this book and conveyed in these gatherings were by and large received positively and sympathetically. I attribute this positivity and sympathy to two factors. But before I touch on them, I want to acknowledge that the very fact that I must explain them here points to the underlying question: How can ideas about reconciliation resonate positively in a society that for years has rejected outright its very possibility? The first factor is Africa, whose people, landscapes, and stories I discuss. The imagination of the Global North perceives Africa as exotic and mysterious, and thus inherently intriguing. The second factor is the illusion of control. In the era before October Seventh, and especially over the last two decades, in the eyes of most Israeli Jews, the Israeli-Palestinian conflict was something that existed but was distant and mostly under control, something that could be put aside or pushed to the back of the mind. If I had to articulate this rationalization, it would sound something like this: "Someday, sometime in the far-off future, so far off it can't even be seen, when the conditions are ripe and there's someone to talk to on the Palestinian side, and after we've tackled other, more urgent issues, we'll address the conflict and then the ideas of reconciliation will be relevant and the cases of South Africa and Rwanda can be our inspiration. So why not listen to talks about reconciliation in the meantime? Such theoretical matters are interesting." This illusion of control naturally sits on the foundations of blindness and repression – more on that later.

Then October Seventh happened. My use of the word "happened" does not imply an event that appeared alchemically, something that emerged out of nothing. Similar to tectonic movements that precede the eruption of a volcano and portend it, there were tectonic movements that preceded October Seventh and could have anticipated it, but they were, by and large, suppressed.

By "October Seventh" I mean the massacre carried out by Hamas in the Israeli communities near the border of Gaza, on army bases, and at a music festival of young men and women. Random passersby were also targeted. Then came the response of Israel in Gaza – if one can call what has been done there, the indiscriminate killing, the destruction, the starving, a response. As is typical of violent conflict, this response would not be contained to this one space, but instead spilled over – to the West Bank, to the war with Hezbollah in Lebanon, and to a volatile, multi-arena war with Iran involving many regional and international actors.

AFTER THE INITIAL, PARALYZING, mind-numbing, all-encompassing shock, which lasted many weeks, and which I will return to, it became clear to me that *On Reconciliation* was not finished, and there was another chapter I would have to write. The sealed membrane enveloping the life-affirming Israeli-Jewish mentality – that is, the part of this mind that does not sanctify holy war, that is, most of it – had been torn open. In this sense, the sounding board against which the book had been echoing had changed, had matured in the sense that it now recognized not only the relevance of dealing with the Israeli-Palestinian conflict by looking at other conflicts, but the necessity of doing so. New audiences were exposed to it and demanded that I clarify the meaning of reconciliation, or even just the meaning of talking about reconciliation, in the new era following October Seventh and the war. Because the world had changed. Here was a world where, to return to the idea of violated space, all fears had been realized. Where waking up could not end the nightmare. Where both Jews and Palestinians – many of whom on both sides unfortunately feel that the right to raise this question is reserved for them and them alone – ask: Is it possible, is it at all reasonable, to talk about reconciliation? In other words: Isn't it obscene to speak about such a thing after everything that's happened?

Well, I'll start with the basics.

October Seventh is what happens when there is no reconciliation, and reconciliation is the only way to prevent it from happening again. As to the question: How is this night different from all other nights, that is, after October Seventh? The answer is: This night – this post–October Seventh darkness – is different from all other nights (which is self-evident, I contend) in that it has impacted every Israeli and every Palestinian, bestowing new urgency on finding a different approach than the one that brought us to the place we're at. The conflict has demonstrated that it will not be suppressed. The equation that previously informed the Israeli-Jewish perception and that of many people across the world no longer computes. According to this old equation, power and a sufficient amount – the minimum necessary, of course – of normal life and the appearance of autonomy for the Palestinians can render the conflict marginal, an issue that only requires occasional confrontations, once every few years, and nothing more. It is now clear that a people's yearning for self-determination cannot be extinguished and that systems based on oppression are unstable. It is now clear, quite simply, that unaddressed problems only get worse.

AN X-RAY OF MY INSIDES would reveal that I have grown a new organ: a pendulum hanging from my larynx, descending down my throat, with a weight at its end that swings from side to side in my chest, a movement that echoes the one between my two states of consciousness: grief and shame. Grief and shame. On one side of this perpetual motion, grief over what has been done to us, the Israelis. Grief over the people who lost their lives, their freedom, the integrity of their bodies, their mental health, their homes, their faith in humanity. Grief over a friend, a woman from a kibbutz near Gaza, a peace activist, who was murdered. Grief over another friend, also a peace activist, whose two parents, themselves peace activists, were murdered. Grief over a colleague who was kidnapped from her home together with her daughter and grandchildren, and whose partner was murdered. Grief over a neighbor whose son was critically injured. I could go on, as there are other people I know firsthand for whom October Seventh was a watershed. Their lives will never be the same again. But I'll stop here. Bottom line, it's all very, very personal.

But then, on the other hand, shame for what has become of us, the Israeli Jews. Shame for the things that have been done and continue to be done in our name. Shame for our hearts that have grown rough and coarse and above all closed up like a fist. Shame for a Gazan friend I made at an Israeli-Palestinian meditation conference for peace a few years ago, with whom I've corresponded several times a week since then, a text exchange dotted with emojis filling the language gap. Right after October Seventh he wrote to me. When the Israeli bombings in Gaza started, I wrote to him. We exchanged hearts and wishes for safety. A week later he sent me videos of his bombed house. After a few days he sent similar videos of his son's house, to which he had fled. A few days later his phone went silent. Shame for a colleague in Gaza with whom, a few years ago, I tried to establish a project to promote food security in the Strip. During all the previous rounds of fighting we maintained interest in each other's well-being. When Hamas fired rockets at Tel Aviv, he wrote to me: Take care of yourself. When Israel bombed Gaza, I wrote to him: Take care of yourself. Shame for two peace activists who escaped from Gaza a few years ago after spending months in a Hamas prison for having ties to Israeli peace organizations. Their families are still in Gaza.

But my shame is older, and layered. One layer, formed before October Seventh, is like an ever-present undercurrent. Because even though it seems that the Israelis and the Palestinians are all swimming – and sometimes drowning – in the murky waters of this painful conflict, the truth is that the power relations between the parties are not symmetrical, not now and not before October Seventh. Yes, both sides abuse their power, but there is a strong side and there is a weak side. And the power wielded by the strong side is immeasurably greater than that wielded by the weak side. And I belong to the strong side. In other words, if I were to ask a person who has nothing to do with the conflict to put aside their identifications and values and refer only to their picture of reality and answer this question, *If you had to choose, would you choose to live in Israel or Gaza?* is there anyone who would choose the second option?

And there is another pendulum. It hangs as if from nowhere, perhaps from the sky, moving from side to side in this space where Jews and Palestinians live and have for generations done horrible things to each other. The existence of each of these people is a matter worth dwelling on for a moment, because although there is no disputing that both Jews and Palestinians live in this space, many on each side refuse to recognize that this fact alone is enough to establish another fact, which is that Jews and Palestinians are in a relationship – whether they like it or not, whether it aligns with their worldview or not. The denial of this relationship is equivalent to the refusal of a person who lives in an apartment building to acknowledge that there is a relationship between himself and the other tenants in the building. It can be good or bad, but it is a relationship nonetheless. Because if one of the neighbors dirties the stairwell, the neighbor who denies this relationship can persist in denying this relationship, but still, when he goes up or comes down the stairs, on his way home or on his way out, his feet will step through trash. And if one of the neighbors plays loud music in the middle of the night, the neighbor who persists in denying this relationship will still find himself lying in bed, unable to fall asleep and unable to explain to himself what these sounds are that fill his acoustic space. In the same vein, a professor at Bethlehem University said to me, when I visited his laboratory, "I can't understand you Israelis. You won't approve the construction of a sewage system in Gaza, so the Gazans pour their sewage into the sea. You think that their shit doesn't reach the beach in Ashkelon, where you swim?" The refusal to recognize this relationship – and in some cases, refusal to recognize the very fact of the other's presence in this space – reflects nothing less than a warped view of reality.

Back to that second pendulum and its perpetual motion through space. On one side the Jews are the victim (and, accordingly, the Palestinians are the victimizer), and on the other side the Palestinians are the victim (and, accordingly, the Jews are the victimizer). A victim, a victimizer. A victim, a victimizer. The central question of the conflict may be whose land this is, but the central question that seems to stand in the way of any attempt to end it is this: Who has the right to claim victimhood and who, as a result, is the victimizer?

The identity of the victim and the victimizer, as viewed by both sides, is, of course, related to the current reality, but no less to the ghosts that haunt this land. Among Jews, October Seventh resonates with pogroms in Europe, and its graphicness – the hunting, the burning of bodies, the dismembering of corpses, rape, children hiding in closets – with the Holocaust. The Israeli-Jewish consciousness was flooded with terror, and it appears that parents, grandparents, and great-grandparents' stories of persecution in exile were awakened in response, filling up this consciousness and eclipsing the sense of protection Israelis thought we had secured in Israel. Whereas among the Palestinians, the war in Gaza and its ripples in the West Bank echo the Nakba. Children and grandchildren of refugees – and sometimes, as in the case of my friend in Gaza who is a 1948 refugee from Haifa – were once again expelled from their homes. There was no one to stop the numbing ease, the unbearable casualness, with which they were cast aside.

It is easy to understand the speed with which both sides, in the blink of an eye, retreated to the position of the victim. The current trauma recalls, on a sensory level of smells and sights and sounds, the previous trauma – personal and collective. This conditioning works on Jews and Palestinians like a spell. However, in order to understand the forces that drive this perpetual motion, this movement between the two sides, each of which is convinced that they, and only they, are the victim, it is not enough to understand the mechanisms of memory and conditioning. Because there is another variable, tied to the benefits that accompany the position of the victim. In other words, it's easy to understand why neither side wants to be the victimizer. But why does everyone long to be the victim?

The obvious part of the answer lies in the fact that the victim naturally receives empathy, solidarity, and sometimes even physical support and assistance. However, there is another, less obvious part, which originates from an intuitive connection that most of us draw between victimhood and righteousness. In the simplest sense and according to the crudest distinction – which in many cases is also false – the "winner" of the title of victim is seen as right and the victimizer as wrong. It is easy to see, then, why victimhood is so desirable, since this link carries with it confirmation of the claims of the victimized party. In the emotional realm, this logic is deciphered as such: Injustice is bad. The one who is wronged is a victim and the one who committed this wrong is a victimizer. Therefore, the one who committed the wrong cannot be right. Hence the victimizer is wrong and the victim is right.

However, the victim-victimizer distinction is a false distinction, because it does not take into account the full complexity of the person in a conflict. In fact, it perpetuates and even deepens one of the more profound, oppressive injustices inflicted on people who are in conflict: it erases their uniqueness. Because a person, each person, is singular and unique, and at the same time a part of the group to which he or she belongs – Israeli Jews and Palestinians in this case. The victim-victimizer distinction affixes a value judgment to him based on the collective to which he belongs, thereby nullifying his stances and choices as a private individual.

The automatic link between victimhood and righteousness distorts reality, which is more complex than the victim-victimizer dichotomy, certainly when you find, as we will see later, that a person can be a victim through his collective affiliation and a victimizer as an individual, and vice versa. This link distorts matters further, since the "winner" of the victim title weaponizes the attendant righteousness against the victimizer, whose characteristics he exaggerates and intensifies, unable to see that there are, always, reasons – not justifications – for this unjust behavior. The victim feels that his victimhood allows him to do things that he could not otherwise justify. A victim position is a sick position. So sick it can blind. So sick that a Palestinian can say, for example, that the Jews brought October Seventh on themselves. So sick that an Israeli Jew can, for example, be blind to the unbelievable historical twist in which her side is starving children in Gaza.

As to the question of who at this point in time in the Israeli-Palestinian conflict is the victim and who is the victimizer, the natural, and perhaps tempting, response would be that the answer depends on one's point of view, although in this era subjectivity is both the foundation on which tolerance is based and, at times, a weapon in the hands of those who reject tolerance altogether. However, I would like to claim that to answer the question of who is the victim and who is the victimizer requires an ability to maintain a complex, multifaceted, and multilayered point of view, an ability that was gradually eroding and seems to have disappeared altogether since October Seventh. Here's what I mean. In the broader context, the Palestinians – under occupation, without political rights, and with unimaginable restrictions on their most basic human rights – are the victim. And Israel, whose boot is on the neck of the Palestinians, is the victimizer. However, on October Seventh, Hamas went so far beyond what is considered acceptable human behavior, even among people immersed in conflict, that from the point of view of the Israeli Jews, the roles were reversed. From the point of view of many Israeli Jews, the Palestinians have lost their "right" to victimhood, and the pendulum of the coveted victimhood has swung to the Israeli side.

This is a position whose logic can be understood, because in the absence of context – assuming a situation without a context is possible, more on that in a moment – whoever is murdered or has had a loved one murdered, is kidnapped or has had a loved one kidnapped, is raped or hunted or forced to witness this is a victim. And whoever murders, kidnaps, hunts, or rapes another person is a victimizer. But a person can, at the same time, belong to a victimized group and be a victimizer as an individual. Conversely, a person can simultaneously belong to a victimizing group and be a victim as an individual. In order to hold this complexity, one must think in a way that is in sharp contrast to the way people usually think in a situation of conflict. One must recognize a person's collective identity and also their private identity, the one that gets lost, because the conflict is a black hole that swallows everything singular and unique about a person, to the point that each and every member of this collective has the same characteristics. Holding this complexity is a great challenge for the parties involved in the conflict, and, as it turns out in this war, for many in the world as well. Too many people seek to express identification with one side or the other and find it difficult to contain the nuances, layers, and uniqueness of the other side. Thus, while it seems to them that they are supporting the "side" with which they identify, in fact they are reinforcing the distorting victim discourse and perpetuating the conflict. It is understandable – but not justifiable – that those who are neck-deep in conflict are overwhelmed by grief and terror to the point that they struggle to see the suffering of the other and, in fact, struggle to see the other at all. But the international supporters of either side should be able to handle complexity and hold it for the sides as a flame of hope and a vital tool for helping the parties extricate themselves from the conflict.

As I write these things about victim-victimizer relations, I carry with me, like a smooth stone one takes home as a souvenir from a special place, another way to understand these relationships, a way I have been repeatedly exposed to in my conversations with people who live in reconciling societies. It is a stage in the relationship between the sides, an evolution that transforms the victim-victimizer opposition so dramatically that it eclipses the simple, common-sense nature of it: by moving away from their roles as victim or victimizer, which the conflict assigned to them, the parties involved make way for a movement in their consciousness as well. This movement enables them to see both themselves and the other more clearly, and more fully. The victim can, for example, recognize in himself those impulses, those dark areas of the soul that until then he attributed only to the victimizers, and will thus be able to imagine a different state of affairs in which he himself would have behaved as they did. And the victimizer can, for example, identify within himself those parts that yielded to the primal impulses of superiority and expansion, and cultivate antibodies against these impulses. There are moments – I witnessed them again and again – when those involved in reconciliation look at the conflict from the other side of it and come to share this understanding: the conflict has exacted a monstrous price from both parties.

THE STRUGGLE BETWEEN ISRAELI JEWS and Palestinians rages in another arena, that of narrative, where the battle revolves around the question of context and more precisely, when, if ever, it is reasonable to disregard it.

As far as the Palestinians are concerned, October Seventh did not take place in a vacuum but in a context where the balance of power is clear: Israel is an occupier and Palestinians in the West Bank, East Jerusalem, and Gaza are waging a struggle against this occupation. The atrocities committed by Hamas – legitimate or not, depending on one's point of view – are part of this struggle. The Israeli-Jewish insistence on ignoring the context is, for Palestinians, a direct continuation of Jewish Israel's longstanding denial of the Israeli-Palestinian conflict and the occupation at its center.

As far as Israeli Jews are concerned, the acts committed on October Seventh were so extreme, so horrifying, that nothing can justify them. Therefore, the very discussion of a context suggests that there might be – even theoretically – mitigating circumstances for these acts. Indeed, in the simplest and most basic way, there is only one answer to the question, "When is rape allowed?" Never.

Interestingly, the math of the Israeli Jews and the Palestinians is similar, but their conclusions are different. And both sides are wrong, because what they are seeking in this is self-justification and sympathy, not moral clarity or a road map to climbing out of the deep, dark pit both sides have fallen into.

> October Seventh + context = a reduction in the severity of October Seventh

Therefore, based on the same equation, Israeli Jews wish to avoid context, while Palestinians wish to emphasize it.

A similar struggle is underway regarding the war in Gaza. In this case, the context is not the occupation but October Seventh, and here the motivations are reversed. From the point of view of Israeli Jews, it is impossible, and inaccurate, to see the war in Gaza except in the context of October Seventh. The war is a reaction, and therefore context is warranted. From the point of view of the Palestinians, the acts that Israel has committed in Gaza are so extreme, so horrific, that nothing can justify them, and therefore the very discussion of context suggests that there might be – even theoretically – mitigating circumstances for these acts. Indeed, in the simplest and most basic way, there is only one answer to the question, "When is it permissible to starve children?" Never. The Palestinians are therefore interested in downplaying the context.

Like the struggle over victimhood, the struggle over context sits on the foundations of another intuitive, and false, link: between context and justification. Thus, while context can, at best, offer an explanation, both sides are mistaken in thinking that it provides legitimacy or permission to do something that under any other circumstances they would not do.

Nevertheless, I would like to argue that context is warranted. Not because it has any implications for one's moral judgment of the events in question. Nothing, not even the occupation, can justify October Seventh. And nothing, not even October Seventh, justifies Israel's actions in Gaza. Context has another value distinct from the question of justification, as it addresses a question that constantly hovers over us all: What will be? Because despite the desire, and perhaps also the instinct, of Israeli Jews to push October Seventh outside the realm of humanity, and of Palestinians to do the same with Israel's actions in Gaza, these acts were not committed in some parallel universe. Unfortunately, they were committed in our universe, a universe where there is a conflict and where resolving it is the only way to prevent such acts from being committed again.

At this point, we must call on our ability to hold complexity: there is context, but while it is weaponized in a conflict state of mind, in the framework of reconciliation, context is what offers us a roadmap to a different future, one where both sides picture reality and experience it at its fullest and richest. Because on the other side of the conflict, different and sometimes contradictory narratives can exist side by side. Through reconciliation, humans can feel their own pain and the pain of others as well, even if they belong to the opposite side. Humans still experience intense and sometimes destructive emotions, because that's how we are – we contain everything, including, thankfully, social and emotional mechanisms of regulation that become sharper and more sophisticated when practiced. Through the process of reconciliation, the energy that was formerly directed toward rebuke and destruction is directed toward healing and rebuilding.

I will touch on the disappearance of complexity later, but first a few more words regarding the charged nature of context, because make no mistake, none of this is easy to swallow. It is not easy to accept the idea that the acts that were committed took place within a framework that can be referred to at all. It seems to me that this is because although October Seventh and the war in Gaza can be explained – but not justified – in terms of the historical context, what the psyche has encountered in them cannot easily be explained in terms of a psychological context. Because the acts committed on October Seventh – sadistic acts whose purpose, so explicitly, was to cause indescribable suffering – are difficult to fit into the ways of thinking we are used to, that is, into the accepted patterns of behavior between human beings, even among those who are in conflict. Similarly, the ways of thinking to which we are accustomed reject unrestrained revenge and apocalyptic scenarios involving starvation, expulsion, and indiscriminate bombing.

Indeed, when the mind meets the indescribable, it rushes to place it in the realm of the abnormal, the deviant – beyond what is considered human. To a place beyond the limits of logic, the only place where such raw and absolute evil goes unopposed and can therefore exist.

The attempt to place evil beyond the limits of logic occurs in an instinctive, survivalist, and also understandable manner, since accepting evil as something that is possible within the scope of what is considered human hollows out the very definition of humanity, emptying it until all that is left is its shell. However, denying the evil in humanity is a fruitless endeavor since it cannot change the fact that this encounter with evil has already happened, has already been burned into the mind. Placing the acts under the heading "inhuman" does not eliminate their reality. In reality, inhuman things were done by human beings.

It's worthwhile to consider the fate of the psyche that remains stuck there, in the lawless and perverse realm where one person can hunt down another, burn them, cut off their limbs, rape them, kidnap them, and do all this while others – sometimes those related to the one being hunted down, burned, cut apart, raped, kidnapped – witness all this. There may lie an explanation – but not a justification – of Israel's unrestrained, unhinged reaction. In other words, a consciousness thrust into a lawless, perverse space tends to react in a lawless, perverse way. After all, indiscriminate killing, mass expulsion, total destruction, and starvation are not acceptable actions, not even in war. They can only be the result of a sickened state of mind in the throes of war's frenzy, a frenzy that should also be considered outside of what is human.

This is a situation where, in practice, the psyche has been suspended. Israeli Jews as well as Palestinians are in such great pain that the psyche cannot bear it, so it urges the body to act, but to act independently of it. Because killing, destroying, razing, expelling, raping, kidnapping, starving are actions that require the psyche to detach itself from the acting body. And this is how Israeli Jews and Palestinians communicate with each other. They appear to speak different languages, but in actuality they communicate with each other in the shared language of soulless action.

DURING MY YEARS working in Africa, I found that when I returned to my life back home, I could convey a bit, a tiny bit, of what I encountered and experienced. Or perhaps more accurately, who I was when I was there. I was able, I think, to provide details and describe situations. For example, I told people about Katanga, a huge shantytown in Kampala, or about Kibera, in Nairobi, both of which are hard to imagine as places where people actually live, the vastness of their size matched only by the degree to which their inhabitants have been abandoned. Shacks stretch to the horizon like an ocean. Children walk around barefoot, their bellies bloated. Sometimes edema, caused by malnutrition, is visible in their legs, arms, and faces. There's no running water or electricity, and sewage flows in the streets. I told people about a young mother, or maybe it was an older sister, who washed a little boy standing naked next to a small tub at the threshold of their shack. There was very little water in the tiny tub, and she dipped a rag in it and wrung it out well before running it over the boy's skin, being careful not to waste a drop. And I told people about a woman who set up a clinic there. She's a public health worker who also functions as a doctor, social worker, and psychologist. People come to her and she does what she can for them, even if, in the absence of medicine, food, and medical equipment, it's simply to let them lie down in her rickety hut, which doesn't even have a door, just a sheet for a partition. And I told people how I stood on a pile of garbage, one of many, since the neighborhoods are dotted with piles of garbage, and I couldn't help but think: humanity is garbage. But I doubt I was able to describe my obliterating, nullifying encounter with a poverty that is both immeasurable and unforgivable. The obliteration and the nullification, these I couldn't convey. Nor the knowledge – which when I stood there couldn't have been more clear to me – that if the world of plenty really cared about its hungry brethren, things would be different.

So here, too, in this text – though I'm not on a garbage heap in Katanga or Kibera, but in my writing nook, in my room, in my city, and in my language – I'll try to convey to those who don't live here something of what living here feels like since October Seventh. I know that my ability to do this is limited. Not only because it is difficult to describe a reality that is unimaginable even for those experiencing it, but also because for many people across the globe my voice as an Israeli Jew has lost its legitimacy.

At this point, my insides become split between different and, at times opposing, identities and identifications. As an Israeli Jew, I feel that the gaze of those uninterested in hearing me reduces me down to the single identity of an Israeli Jew, and flattens me altogether. Under this gaze and this silencing, being a woman, mother, writer, and human rights and reconciliation activist is meaningless. My critical view of the society in which I live and of myself is meaningless, as are the solidarity and empathy with which I try to orient my life. As someone who defines herself as a humanist, I actually understand the emotional and moral impulse of those who feel that today's Israel represents values that are unacceptable to humanism in the simplest and most basic sense: equality between human beings whoever and wherever they may be. I understand the desire to say to Israeli Jews: "You have lost your right to attention and compassion; come back to us when you wake up from the delusion that your behavior is legitimate." However, as someone who researches reconciliation and writes about it, I know that when zooming in, nuances and complexities are revealed, and I know that silencing people on the basis of group affiliation (ethnic, religious, gender, etc.) actually deepens and reinforces conflict, it doesn't bring its solution closer. Deeming an entire side illegitimate delegitimizes as well its reconciliation and equal rights activists, that is, the very people who want and can change reality, along with all the many others who want with all their heart to see the conflict end but still struggle to see how this might happen. If there is anything that my encounter with reconciling societies taught me, it is that reality can be changed, because it is human beings who create it, or at least significant parts of it. Human beings know how to change, know how to transform as individuals, and know how to transform as a collective.

Survivors of October Seventh said that while they were hiding – in shelters, closets, garbage cans, in holes they dug in the ground and buried themselves in almost completely – their babies and their dogs were silent. They didn't cry, they didn't bark. In fact, they didn't move. They felt – instinctually, in their cells, deep inside the same mechanism that makes them a living organism – that they were in grave danger. They experienced a survival response: in the absence of the ability to fight or to flee, there was nothing left for them to do but freeze. This paralysis – before it tumbled in the other direction, into wild, unrestrained action – was everywhere.

Inside me too. October Seventh left me speechless. Not only in the physical sense of my jaw locked and my mouth closed, but also in regards to my inner voice, which was shocked and muted in the face of the horror, which silenced my ability to write as well. Again and again, I found myself bringing my hand under my chin to lift my jaw, which constantly seemed to be dropping in response to the sights, the voices, the information that flowed into me. I could do nothing to stop it, because it came from everywhere – from the news, from conversations, from texts, from the testimony of people I knew. And this information was so extreme, so disturbing, that it activated every skeptical mechanism I had, so that when I was able to say something, it was mostly: "What?" And if there was someone next to me, I would turn to him and ask, "Is this really what that person just said? Did you hear that too?" Or, "Is this what you're seeing in that picture? Do you see it too?" I was sure I wasn't seeing, hearing, or reading right, or maybe that's simply what I wanted to believe – that I couldn't see well, hear well, or read right. These things went beyond what the mind can grasp, and this is what the mind does when it encounters things that lie beyond its grasp: it pushes them away or looks for confirmation from other sources.

But there was nowhere to escape to. The experience was overflowing with graphic horrors and loss, much like the air can be saturated with dust or moisture that clings to everything, sticks to the body, and penetrates the mind. And this experience was drained of those things that are essential to existence: vitality and logic, until it took on the form of death and irrationality. The public sphere resembled a house in which people sit shiva. Feelings were exposed and raw. It appeared that the seam separating people's inner speech – that discourse resonating internally with coherence and reason – from their speech with others – where the same things suddenly hover in a hallucinatory space – had been undone. People stood in the streets and cried, or walked and cried, or sat and cried, or paid at the cash register in the supermarket and cried. People ran into each other in the street and fell apart on each other's shoulders. Or reached out to caress someone's shoulder or arm, to offer comfort, even when that someone was a perfect stranger. Fragments of conversation that float in the acoustic space of our cellular age suddenly changed. Normally, a person walks down the street, passes people, and hears things like: "I'm stopping by the supermarket and then I'll come, OK?" Or: "You don't want to know about the traffic." Now you'd walk down the street and were exposed to bits of dialogue that in any other context would have seemed impossible: "Their two children! Do you hear me? They found pieces of the daughter; the son was kidnapped!" Or: "There's nothing left of them, just soot; there wasn't even anything left of their glasses."

One day I was standing at a crosswalk. Next to me stood a young woman pushing a stroller with a baby in it. She was wearing dark sunglasses, and underneath, tears were running down her cheeks and face. They flowed off her jawline like a waterfall over a cliff. Her expression was frozen. Nothing moved except for the tears wetting her shoes. Normally I would have asked her if I could help somehow. But there was nothing so unusual about what she was doing. So we stood side by side, both of our shoes stained with tears. The pain was so raw and so exposed, so wild, that public space felt like a butcher shop, and the people filling it were bloody pieces of meat, hanging on hooks or lying, cut wide open, on butcher blocks. A few weeks into the war, reality echoed the feeling of the butcher shop and those pieces of meat. In those days, many of the murdered had already been identified, and from the videos released by Hamas it was clear that many had been kidnapped, but there were still many who were missing. It was then that various birds of prey known to feed on corpses entered the frame of our hallucinatory reality. The Nature Reserve Authority had attached transmitters to their legs to monitor their flight and health, and now in the areas where they circled the air rescue forces would search and find bodies, and parts of bodies.

And throughout this time I saw, and still see, the sign that a father, whose daughter was kidnapped, posted on the street: "This could have been your daughter." And I knew then and I know now: it's true.

TWO WEEKS AFTER October Seventh, I was in the car. The ground entry of the Israeli army into Gaza had not yet begun. Every day we learned of people who had gone from the status of missing to the status of dead or kidnapped. Every few hours a siren tore through the membrane surrounding reality. It once seemed – incorrectly – that this membrane could keep reality intact. People ran to shelters or, in their absence, to stairwells, and if they were outside they lay down on the road or on the sidewalk and covered their heads with their hands. I was driving and daydreaming at the same time, a state in which the imagination does what it wants with the mind, and the laws are the laws of the dream world even though you know it's a dream. Your consciousness signals: "You know it's not real. Don't be confused." But in those days what I had to remind myself was precisely the opposite: "You are not dreaming. You know this is real. Don't be confused." The radio, like the television, became an open channel that broadcast nonstop reports about missing persons and bodies and hostages and in between played sad songs as a lament. And suddenly my attention was caught by a man running on the side of the road. He was facing me; he ran toward me and then passed by and continued on, and all the while I followed him with my gaze to make sure that I was indeed correctly deciphering what I was seeing, because although I remained unmoved, another part of me was telling me that there was something wrong with this picture. Exercise clothes for his body, running shoes for his feet, and a pineapple resting on his head. A real man, a real pineapple. A scene that seems to have been taken out of a hallucination, but at that moment it struck me as something that was utterly explicable, because in an insane reality, what's wrong with a man running on the side of the road with a pineapple on his head during a war?

I dwell on the man and the pineapple because it seems to me that what defines insanity is not the crazy details, but rather those same details that, within a ruptured reality, suddenly become normal and seem sane. Thus, just as a person visiting a psychiatric ward will not be dumbfounded if they stumble upon a conversation between two people in which one is telling the other, as a trivial matter, that the TV announcer spoke to them and ordered them to do something, so I was, for the very first time, encountering parts of myself that were newly indifferent to what in any other context would have raised a dozen red flags inside me. A friend told me she was looking into how she could get her hands on cyanide, in case Hamas or Hezbollah reach the center of the country. She's not willing to go through something like that, she said, she's not willing to be hunted down. And that seemed reasonable to me. A friend told me that he tested the escape routes from the balcony of their apartment on the second floor, that he practices this escape from the balcony to a tree in the yard of their building and from the tree to a stone wall, and that he taught his daughters how to do this. And this seemed to me a logical course of action. A friend placed a knife in every room of the house. If terrorists come, she said. And I thought to myself that in the event that such terrorists come to her home, a kitchen knife would not help her, yet her desire to have something to hold on to seemed not unreasonable to me.

This is a pattern that repeats itself among people in conflict, and certainly in war: the consciousness operates in survival mode, reality is misread, and people's actions are limited to grabbing on to whatever is possible, sometimes while knowing – on one level or another – that the thing you're grasping is nothing more than a twig floating in the ocean drowning you. South Africans, black and white, and Rwandans, Hutu and Tutsi, told me that they look at who they were then, in the midst of the conflict, as people who acted as automatons, who fulfilled a role assigned to them, and who did so with very little hesitation. Again and again, I was impressed by their ability, with the passing of time, to see that a similar pattern had controlled those who had been their enemies, something they couldn't see during the conflict itself.

MY JAW CLENCHED, my fingers stiffened, and my guts cramped until my inner speech became nothing more than a faint stutter. Beyond the limitations inherent in trying to convey an experience that is horrifically overwhelming, in particular to someone outside of it, within hours another difficulty became clear. The war was claiming not only lives and homes, physical and mental wholeness, and hope – it was also claiming complexity.

Murder and bombing and dismemberment and kidnapping and expulsion and rape and tunnels and abuse and missiles and refugee camps and hunger were like a sharp knife cutting reality up into rigid and opaque categories. Reality is normally a living, breathing thing, something layered and multifaceted. But thinking with these new categories required deleting and discarding huge amounts of raw material the mind transforms into "reality." So much gets left out. It is difficult to characterize those mental fragments that wind up on the cutting-room floor of the mind, but it seems to me that it is everything not contained in a simple answer to this question: Are you Israeli-Jewish (or on the side of) or are you Palestinian (or on the side of)? Being a teacher or a doctor or a parent or a brother or a friend, one who likes music or computer games or sports or literature does not make the cut. All these remain outside the national-ideological costume that a person is now forced to wear. In this way, people become less human and more like caricatures.

In the same way, discourse also became a slave to the tyranny of simplification. It has become superficial and dogmatic, to the point that often it does not satisfy the most basic definition of communication: the exchange of information, ideas, and feelings. In this space, characterized by intellectual laziness, speech is not speech but a slap in the face, and language operates only in a collective register: those who are "in favor" of Israel are required to be shocked by what Hamas did on October Seventh (not difficult) but also to silence any criticism of the intensity of Israel's military response in Gaza and turn a blind eye to the occupation (difficult). Those who are "in favor" of the Palestinians are required to be horrified by the war that Israel is waging on Gaza (not difficult) but also to minimize somehow the severity of the atrocities that took place on October Seventh (difficult), sometimes to the point of denying them.

For Israeli Jews and Palestinians, suspicion and self-righteousness dominate every exchange. Each of them remains in the state of mind of a touch-me-not, a climbing plant so sensitive that it is enough to pass one's hand over its leaves for them to fold up and close. Both sides are so overwhelmed that they cannot tolerate complexity, since complexity requires the recognition of nuance and a willingness to contain contradictions. It requires questioning absolute statements and what appear to be unquestionable truths. Sometimes this touch-me-not state of mind also demands proof of loyalty or the search for its apparent absence. Any deviation from what fits neatly within the available categories is proof enough: there is a stain on this person. Time and time again, I found myself talking to Israeli Jews about the horrifying reality in Gaza and immediately being required to state that there can be no leniency in response to the acts of October Seventh, as if the mere inclusion of the Palestinian disaster in a conversation about ours minimizes the horror. Again and again, I found myself talking to Palestinians and seeing that my shock at October Seventh made them impatient, as if the crimes of the Israeli Jews over the years somehow justified what had been done. For many, both Jews and Palestinians, the very comparison between the suffering of one people and the suffering of another is offensive, unimaginable, intolerable, and whoever makes such a comparison is required to prove their innocence. In this context, innocence means not challenging these rigid categories.

However, there are situations in which a consciousness wishing to preserve its humanity must break away from the categories of "us" and "them," must guard against such categorizing at all costs. These are situations when all a consciousness must do is call upon its power of empathy, which transcends the categories of "us" and "them."

For example, a man of about thirty years old. Children and adults are gathered around him, one of whom takes a video and a little later sends it out to the world from Gaza. In the background, smoke billows from the aftermath of a bomb, but those present pay no attention to it, as if it were a trivial matter, as if people and bombs normally inhabit the same space. The man is holding a baby girl in his hands. Maybe it's his daughter, we don't know, but that's the sense that comes through and that's the expression on his face, the expression of a man who has lost everything. The baby is wearing a pink and gray outfit with white stars. The man holds her a little away from his body, his arms outstretched before him, the baby faces the people surrounding them. He is running through the rubble. Everything is gray, dusty. People approach them and retreat, approach and retreat. Two girls stand side by side, witnessing the event. They cry. No one goes to comfort the girls because all attention is on the man and the baby. The baby's face is smooth, peaceful. Her eyes are closed. If it weren't for her limbs hanging loosely from her like a doll and her head drooping to the side in an exaggerated manner, one might think she were asleep. The man shouts her name and age: Zeina (Arabic for "beautiful" or "beloved")! Five months old! Zeina! A paramedic enters the frame and gently takes her from the man's hands and enters an ambulance. He sits down, the baby in his lap. He gazes at the baby and strokes her head. He lifts one of her eyelids and looks, swallowing saliva. Checks her pulse and raises his head. He cradles her with immeasurable tenderness. She is dead.

For example, a seventeen-year-old boy. He wears a white tank top and shorts. His neck is adorned with a chain, and a butterfly is tattooed on the back of his right arm, as if there is room for beauty in all this. He has a hint of a mustache and is barefoot. The GoPro camera mounted on the head of a Hamas terrorist broadcasts the event live. From time to time, one of the terrorists enters the frame, sometimes the automatic weapon aimed at the boy pops in. They walk along the paths of the kibbutz, the boy first, followed by a group of terrorists. House by house, the boy is sent to call for the neighbors to come out, and when they come out at the sound of their neighbor's familiar voice, the terrorists murder them. Right in front of his eyes. They arrive at another house. The boy tries to save the neighbors by pretending no one is there. "Where is everybody?" asks the terrorist. "I don't know," the boy replies, but they enter the house. The boy continues trying. He opens doors to rooms and closets, as if to offer proof that the place is empty, and all the while automatic guns are pointed at him. They reach the door of the safe room and the boy demonstrates that it is locked and then makes a there's-nothing-to-do-nobody's-here gesture. It's hard to know if he believes he'll be able to convince the armed men surrounding him, but he tries. But the terrorists press him, so he calls out to the neighbors: "Open the door! Come out!" The door doesn't open. Maybe the people sitting inside know what's going on. There's no way to know. Several shots are fired at the door, behind which parents and three children sit on the floor in the dark, without making a sound, while the father holds the door handle in a desperate attempt to protect his family. But after the shots the door opens. The older daughter, eighteen, is lying in a pool of blood. She's dead. One of the terrorists takes the mother's phone, and from this moment on, the whole incident is broadcast live on her Facebook page. Their relatives watch on screens: the mother sitting on the floor with her two young children, who are crying and repeatedly asking if it's true, is their sister really dead? The father sits next to them, his head drooping in the lifeless posture of a man who has given up, his hands covered in the blood of his dead daughter, who is still lying in a puddle of her own blood. He says nothing. A few hours later, the father will be kidnapped, while the boy next door, after finishing the role he is forced to perform as an accomplice of the murderers, will himself be murdered, along with his mother and her partner. The partner's daughters will be kidnapped.

The man and the baby in Gaza embody the absolute arbitrariness of indifferent violence. In an act that could not be any less personal, and therein lies its monstrosity, the fate of human beings deemed dispensable is determined by aerial bombardment. Whereas the boy and the family embody the other end, the highly personal, since the horror occurring there happened in a space in which there was communication between the boy, the family, and the terrorists. Words, looks, physical gestures, breath were all exchanged. But regardless of these differences, complexity calls on us to let the story of the father holding his dead baby, or that of the boy who is forced to cooperate with the murder of his neighbors, bypass the rigid patterns of "us" and "them" and penetrate one's consciousness. And it is then that empathy, which embraces complexity and rejects the limitations inherent in "us" and "them," can arise. As I have argued throughout this book, an absence of empathy is never limited to "them." It infects that reference known as "us," defiling and polluting it.

Too many Israeli Jews react by shrugging their shoulders at the indescribable suffering that Israel inflicts on Gaza. Too many Palestinians react by shrugging their shoulders at the indescribable suffering that Hamas inflicts on Israel. It's senseless to claim that Jews and Palestinians were born defective, lacking the capacity for empathy. Empathy is an innate ability, but living in conflict, living life in survival mode, consumes it. By contrast, empathy is an ability that develops through the process of reconciliation, which, in addition to being life-enhancing and allowing normalcy, also grows and expands one's consciousness.

WAS IT POSSIBLE to anticipate October Seventh? The painful answer is yes, for two reasons. One concerns Israeli-Jewish society, the other its relations with the Palestinians. And the two reasons are connected and feed off each other. Put differently: human consciousness is a slippery thing. It knows not only how to deceive others, it knows how to deceive itself.

First, Israeli-Jewish society. In terms of collective consciousness and collective emotional life, the months leading up to October Seventh set the stage. After four election campaigns, Netanyahu – a man lacking inhibition or moral backbone – was unable to form a government, so he made an alliance with racist, messianic, and anti-democratic parties on the right, establishing a government whose agenda was to annex Palestinian territories, suffocate (a far-from-perfect) Israeli democracy, affirm Jewish supremacy, and above all, help Netanyahu, who was accused of bribery, fraud, and breach of trust, to evade prison. Toward these ends, restraints were undone and inhibitions were eliminated. For forty weeks, protests that often swelled to hundreds of thousands filled the streets demanding a stop to the government's actions. A smell of disintegration was in the air, the collapse of the most basic social agreements and of state institutions whose job is to serve the public but that were now oppressing it instead. In the most concrete sense, the state's institutions were being smashed and desecrated. The state reneged on its responsibility toward its citizens, and on October Seventh it indeed became clear that those who were supposed to protect did not protect and those who were supposed to act did not act. Their attention, resources, and presence were elsewhere, serving other interests, not those of the public. In effect, the state had ceased to exist. Civil society took it upon itself to fill the void and functioned in place of the state until it somewhat returned to its senses, but the feeling of abandonment remained.

All this helps to explain why October Seventh could have been expected. Everything was visible: the trust that had cracked, the social fabric that had frayed, all the attention that had been given to the struggle over the character of the state. The gate to the soft underbelly of the State of Israel was wide open. All Hamas had to do was implement the plans it had been working on for years. Israeli-Jewish society was so self-absorbed and so stubborn in its unwillingness to look at the reality in which the Israeli-Palestinian conflict continued to fester that it did not anticipate what was coming. Dr. Hussein Fawzi, one of Egypt's greatest intellectuals, said in a conversation with the Israeli writer Haim Guri at his home in Cairo in December 1977, shortly after Sadat's visit to Jerusalem: "If Israeli intelligence had read Egyptian poetry written after '67, it would have known that October '73 was inevitable. Any good intelligence officer must read poetry." But how could Israeli Jews read Palestinian poetry if they wouldn't even look at Palestinians to begin with?

Second, the relationship of Israeli-Jewish society with the Palestinians. In an essay titled "This Was Auschwitz," Primo Levi writes: "We know other definitions of fascism, but it seems more precise, and more consistent with our specific experience, to define as fascist all regimes and only those which deny, in theory or in practice, a basic equality of rights among all human beings." During the months of the government-led judicial coup and the struggle against it, it became clear, once again, that the Israeli-Jewish mainstream was not interested in engaging with the Israeli-Palestinian conflict, believing that it could afford not to engage with it. At the demonstrations in favor of (a flawed but still standing) democracy, many demonstrators found it difficult to accept the call to look at the occupation for what it is, or, in other words, to recognize that a democracy that holds millions without rights is not really a democracy, and that it was the occupation that enabled the judicial overhaul. Democracy and occupation cannot coexist; so it should come as no surprise that the racist-messianic camp sought to abolish the former. In this regard, it can be said that the occupation conquered Israel.

SOMETIMES A LAKE SPEAKS, getting wet even those who don't enter it. That's what Lake Kivu did to me. I first got to know the Rwandan side of it, which I wrote about in Chapter 4. But it was when I got to know it from the other side, in the Democratic Republic of Congo, that it stayed with me, just as bits of reality sometimes remain because they give voice to what has been silenced. Every time I experience the Israeli-Jewish insistence on suppressing the conflict, I return to the lake, whose incredible beauty brings to mind nymphs and heavenly beings. Its presence exceeds that of a body of water, even a large one, and possesses mythical qualities. The residents of the area treat the lake with awe, as a silent giant that must be dealt with carefully, lest it wake from its slumber. A little after dark, dozens of long, narrow fishing boats pull out of their anchorage, flickering like birthday candles on a large, endless cake. Kerosene lamps mounted on them function like flutes from Hamelin, attracting tiny fish like the piper summoned rats. The fish are gathered up in nets and spread out the next day on land to dry in the sun and be sold to those who can afford them.

"Can you swim in the lake?" I asked a colleague after a few days there, because I hadn't seen anyone in the water.

"Of course you can," he replied.

But a few more days passed, and I still hadn't seen anyone in the lake. It dawned on me that I hadn't asked the right question. After all, the answer I received was a literal answer to the question I had asked. You can indeed swim in the lake. No one will stop you.

"Do people swim in the lake?" I asked again, rephrasing my question.

"No. A minute or two after entering the water, the methane begins to take effect. You feel very tired. Your arms and legs become heavy, and you can't swim. You can even drown."

In the lakeside city of Bukavu and in nearby villages as well, the evil wind, *mazuku* in Swahili, comes up occasionally in conversation. Someone mentions a person who fell asleep by the lake and died in his sleep because of the *mazuku*. Another talks about the *mazuku* that may or may not come, only God knows. I collected such sayings. At first, I filed them away in my mind and in my notebook for future contemplation, as I do in situations when I only have time to act, not process. Later on I did some reading and found out that until the 1980s, people – mainly the *wazungu* ("whites" in Swahili), of course – used the term to refer to a local legend, according to which every few hundred years, without warning, an evil wind would rise from the lake and kill all the surrounding humans and animals. As long as it was possible to treat the *mazuku* as a legend, and especially one that connects the physical world to the world of spirits, a casual approach to this mythological threat from the lake seemed reasonable.

However, based on additional reading and conversations with local colleagues, professionals, and representatives of international aid organizations, I learned that the picture had changed. The *mazuku* passed from the realm of legend to that of science in 1984, when thirty-seven people died, just like that, near Lake Monoun in Cameroon. Two years later, 1,700 people died in the same mysterious way in a village near Lake Nyos, also in Cameroon. A seventy-eight-foot-high tsunami brought attention to the lake as the source of the calamity, if not as the actual cause of death. The dead bodies, which showed signs of suffocation, pointed to the cause: the waters of the lakes – now known as "overturning lakes" prone to limnic eruptions – are brimming with carbon dioxide. Volcanic activity or even a particularly strong storm or landslide can cause the gas to be released into the air. Such a cloud, odorless and colorless, kills all humans and animals nearby. Indeed, an evil wind.

The solution to the mystery of the *mazuku* came from the west of the continent, from Cameroon, where work has since been done to drain the carbon dioxide. The two lakes are now considered safe. In contrast, Lake Kivu remains a particularly daunting instance of this phenomenon. It is much larger than the two Cameroonian lakes, and its carbon dioxide deposits are much greater. If that weren't enough, it is also saturated with methane, another deadly gas that is colorless and odorless as well. Two million people live around this ticking time bomb called Lake Kivu. If it overturns, they will die.

And yet they live there. How can that be? The first answer is related to the financial situation of most of the people who live there. Poverty reduces a person's degree of freedom, in this case their ability to choose where to live. However, this is not a sufficient answer because there are people of means living in the area too. They could move away, but they choose to remain. So it may be that the reason they continue to live near this volatile lake is the same reason we in Israel-Palestine continue to live with the ticking time bomb of the conflict: we repress reality.

I would like to mention in this context that on the Rwandan side of the lake – a country where, unlike the Democratic Republic of Congo, there is significant government oversight – work has been done to convert the toxic gas reserves into energy. That is, they observed the reality, defined the problem, and dealt with it by turning something with destructive potential into something positive. There is such a thing as the opposite of repression. Well, on October Seventh our lake – that is, the conflict – burst open. This thing that most Israeli Jews did not want to see, or saw but thought they could control, has exploded in our faces. If there is anything positive that can be said about what has happened since then, it is that the repression is gone. The elephant is in the room; you can see him, and you can feel the room shake with his every step.

A FEW MONTHS INTO THE WAR, a friend told me: "In the first month after October Seventh, a terrible thing happened to me. I wanted everyone in Gaza to die. I looked in the mirror and saw something terrible. I saw who I had become."

Conflict and its most extreme manifestation, war, bring out the bad in people, not the good. This is an eternal truth in the sense that it is true for all societies, at all times and in all places. War releases inhibitions and allows raw, primal impulses to dominate completely. War perfects the mental acrobatics required to justify this way of being, to look away from the results and be moved by the only thing that human consciousness can, in its distress, grasp while fighting: manifestations of heroism and the unity of "us."

But the cannons will fall silent. The war will end. All wars end. And when it ends, we will be left with its remains: with the dead, injured, and traumatized, and with hollow slogans like "total victory" and "from the river to the sea." And in the silence that follows the storm, both sides will come to see that they are poorer in their humanity. They will be forced to break through the fortified walls they have built around their consciousness, just as humans in every time and place have had to, walls whose impregnability was well described by Marek Edelman, one of the commanders of the Warsaw Ghetto Uprising. Three decades later, by which time he was an innovative cardiologist in Poland, he told the journalist and writer Hanna Krall about the transports in the ghetto. He related how he stood for six weeks, day after day, at the entrance to the *Umschlagplatz* (the transit station), while four hundred thousand people passed him on their way to the trains. Edelman said that the Germans passed out "numbers of life," and whoever received one was guaranteed to stay off the train. Thus, all the people in the ghetto had only one goal: to get such a number. But then the Germans also took those who had a number. Then workers in the factories who knew how to use a sewing machine were allowed to live, so people were willing to pay any amount for one, because they believed that it had the power to save their lives. But a little later, the Germans also took those who managed to get a sewing machine. In the end, says Edelman, the Germans announced that they would distribute bread to anyone who volunteered to board a train to work. "Do you know what bread in the ghetto meant?" he asked Krall. "Because if you don't know, you will never understand why thousands would voluntarily choose to travel with this bread to Treblinka." What Edelman relates is unimaginable: people stood in line in groups of four, took the bread, and boarded the trains. However, what is even more amazing, more impossible to comprehend, is that in 1942 they sent someone from the ghetto to figure out what was happening with the shipments. He returned and reported that every day a train full of people would enter Treblinka and return empty, and that there was no food supply reaching the camp. He didn't merely tell them; these things were also published in the ghetto newspaper. But people didn't believe the things they were told to their face, nor did they believe the article. "Are you crazy? They're sending us with bread to die? They're willing to waste all that bread?" The lack of food was so severe, consciousness took its form. A situation where someone would waste bread could not pass the gate of such a consciousness, much like the possibility of reconciliation is stopped at the gate of a consciousness that is shaped by and only knows conflict. The residents of the Warsaw Ghetto were unfortunately doomed no matter what they did. Take the bread, don't take the bread, you are going to eventually wind up on a train. But in our case, there is a way out. There is a key to the gate of our consciousness. We must accept the key of reconciliation to release ourselves from the prison of conflict in which we have been confined for too long.

Since the release of *On Reconciliation* in Hebrew, I have been giving lectures and workshops on the subject to audiences with diverse political and religious views. Often, I am asked by someone in the audience: "Do you think we too will have to go through a disaster before we get our act together?" Before October Seventh I would answer: "I don't know, I hope not." But here it is, a disaster has happened to us – to Israelis and to Palestinians. What happens in the absence of reconciliation has happened to us.

A FEW WEEKS INTO THE WAR, still cloaked in muteness, I dreamed that I was kidnapped to Gaza. In my dream I tried to convince my captors to give me a notebook and something to write with.

"Every day I'll let you see what I write," I offered, in an attempt to allay their suspicions in the face of my strange request. "That way you'll know I'm not revealing anything to anyone," I told them. "You must have someone here who reads Hebrew," I continued in these surreal negotiations taking place in the damp tunnels, illuminated by a faint light. "And if not, I'll write in English."

My sense that in some way, however much imagined, writing would save me, brought words back to me and me to them. I was returned to writing, which at its best is a container for complexity, for humanity, for life. Those materials are the building blocks of the space that has disappeared, and those are the materials out of which it will be rebuilt. Eternal truths are carved on these building blocks: Human beings are part of their group of affiliation, and they are also singular, unique individuals. Nothing good will grow from the subjugation of a person, just as nothing good will grow from the subjugation of a society. The consciousness of individuals can transform completely and so can the consciousness of societies. The South Africans, the Rwandans, the Israelis and the Egyptians, the French and the Germans, the Irish and the British, and even the Germans and the Jews did it – it is possible.

The darkness of war makes it difficult to read the writing on these building blocks, and the truths written on them are difficult to digest, since they undermine war's basic assumptions and work against its expanding, seemingly inevitable nature. War, like a disease, occupies one's entire consciousness and claims it as its own. But the darkness will fade and the light will shine again. Because conflicts end. It's in their nature. The only question is when, and at what cost, and on which side we will find ourselves at the end: the side that viewed conflict as an inescapable necessity, or the side that imagined a future in which reconciliation replaces conflict, and worked to make this a reality.

Acknowledgments, Sources, and Inspirations

THE PEOPLE whose conversations I presented here generously and openly shared their personal experiences, memories, and thoughts with me. Often their motivation for these conversations was the same as mine: to try to understand this complex, elusive, and unfinished thing known as reconciliation. Each of them walked with me on the challenging and at times incomprehensible path of observing the process and themselves, despite the pain it caused them and the inner conflicts in which they often found themselves. Their choice of reconciliation, an ongoing choice that reality repeatedly puts to the test, is an inspiration to me. To all these people I offer a big, emotional thank you.

Along with these individuals, I was helped by the book *Tomorrow Is Another Country* by Allister Sparks, which narrates the behind-the-scenes of apartheid's end and the amazing human engine that drove this process; the book *Rwanda 1994: Genocide in the "Land of a Thousand Hills"* by Benjamin Neuberger, which explains the details of this genocide's horror; Susan Sontag's *Regarding the Pain of Others*, which drew my attention to the subject of America's commemoration – or lack thereof – of slavery.

I also gained much important assistance from various newspapers and websites, including the *Guardian*, *Financial Times*, *New York Times*, *Independent*, *Spectator*, BBC, *Haaretz*, and *Afrikan*.

The website of the Truth and Reconciliation Commission of the South African Ministry of Justice offers transcriptions and visuals of its deliberations; I also consulted the Truth and Reconciliation Commission's Final Report, the Rwandan government's Rwanda Genocide Archive, the museums of

Robben Island and District 6 in South Africa, and the Kigali Genocide Memorial in Rwanda.

The quote by Jean Cocteau is from *The Journals of Jean Cocteau*, translated into English by Wallace Fowlie. Hila Lahav edited the original Hebrew edition of *On Reconciliation*. After October Seventh and the war on Gaza, Todd Hasak-Lowy said to me: "Now is the time to translate the book." He translated it and then edited the additional chapter "Reconciliation After October Seventh." I'm thankful for the deep intellectual, emotional, and moral exchange with both of them.

The human complexity at the center of reconciliation, along with the moral questions it raises, have occupied my intellectual, emotional, and physical worlds as long as I can remember. It was a part of my upbringing in the home of my peace-building parents, Uri and Aliza Savir. However, it was my encounter with Africa that illuminated the possibility of looking at our conflict through other, very personal eyes of people whose stories and insights might, hopefully, escape the flattening, calcifying effects of the clichés with which we have become accustomed to thinking about ourselves and our partners in this conflict (assuming that clichés allow thinking at all).

I probably wouldn't have come to Africa in the first place if it weren't for the humanitarian project JustSpirulina, and I would like to take this opportunity to thank Ze'ev Degani, who came up with the idea and inspired some Israeli high-school students to act in the world out of a sense of human solidarity and personal responsibility.

And I would like to offer a special thanks to one of the students involved in this initiative, a student who generously shared with me the potential she identified in this project, and who opened the door for me to be a part of it: my daughter, Anouk (Savir-Kadmon) Leshem.

Noam, my first reader and first everything. My children, Lenny, Miki, Anouk, and Alon, are the reason that all of this matters.